Foreword

This book is about happiness, choice, and change.

Statistics show that many young people struggle to find a life of solid happiness. This is how I define happiness as something that is long-lasting and resilient. It is rare to be robustly happy by chance.

Happiness can be your choice. You have the power to make this choice. However, you will need strategies and knowledge before you can achieve happiness. Children rely heavily on their parents and other important adults for well-being when they are young. As they get older, children need to be able to make a happy life for themselves. It is important to give them the tools, knowledge, strategies, and resources they need to succeed in this endeavor.

Children look up to the adults they admire. If you want your children and students to be happy, the most important thing you can do is to model the behavior you want.

Eight precepts are included in the Modeling Happiness program. They are based upon scientific research. A precept is a principle that can be applied to your life. Each precept is intended to enhance your knowledge of supporting science and to provide strategies for putting it into practice.

This book was written primarily for parents and teachers to help them raise happy children. However, the principles can be applied to all people and organizations. These precepts can be just as important for employees and managers of companies as they can for teachers.

You can make a difference in the world by learning more about positive emotions and becoming an example of happiness.

Acknowledgements

It is said that every person has at least one book. However, to make a book a success, you need a team that supports you. A few of my book-writing friends would be nice to recognize.

Alionka Polanco is my first thank-you. She suggested that I write this book during a half-day coaching session. Her spark was what pushed me to action.

My editor Emily Swan and my psychologist consultant Gordon Rose, thank you. They make my thoughts logical and understandable to others. These two sets of eyes make a manuscript more valuable.

Sandy Magee from Red Sand Creative designed the cover. His creativity and skills are incredible and he is so easy to work alongside.

I want to thank everyone who supported my project. Although you are too many to name, know that your support and encouragement were crucial in the creation and completion of this book. I am fortunate to have such wonderful people in my daily life.

Last but not least, I want to thank my family, especially my children and parents, for being there with me on this journey. I am grateful to you for being there with me in the good and bad times, and for your love and support.

Section I –
Building a Foundation

Happiness & Positive Psychology

Happiness can mean different things to everyone, so let's start by clarifying what I mean when talking about happiness.

Happiness can be described as the umbrella that encompasses all positive feelings or emotions. You can substitute happiness with joy, contentment or satisfaction if you prefer. I don't want anyone to get lost in semantics. This book is about teaching skills that will help you live a life that is more positive than negative.

Scientists struggled to understand how to measure emotions when positive psychology was just beginning. How can you tell if someone is happy? What can you do when there is no way to define happiness?

Ed Diener found a solution to this problem when he coined the term "subjective well being". This means that people can self-evaluate their happiness and not leave it up to scientists.

This way of thinking doesn't care what emotion you feel or whether others agree with it. You can be content if you feel happy. If you feel stressed, you will be in a negative state of well-being. This idea will be explored further in the section on Perception.

Psychology was originally a discipline that studied mental illness. The goal of psychology research was to find ways to make people with mental illness live happier lives. Positive psychology broke with tradition. Armed with both a definition of emotion and a strategy for measuring emotion, positive psychology was ready and willing to learn more about the mental health of mentally healthy people.

Martin Seligman, the American Psychology Association's president in 1998, was the breakthrough moment for this discipline. He was a strong advocate of this type of psychology and decided it was time to study mentally healthy individuals and find new ways to make them happier.

Positive psychology research has seen a surge in studies and discoveries since its announcement. These scientific discoveries are the foundation for the strategies and precepts in this book. I will be sharing the results of relevant research studies throughout.

Why Happiness is Important

Since Martin Seligman's call for positive psychology to be recognized as science, thousands of studies have been conducted. Psychologists discovered that people who feel a constant sense of well-being in life have many advantages over those who are unhappy.

Research shows that happy people have many benefits, including the obvious benefit of feeling better about themselves and their lives:

* More successful
* Make friends more often, have stronger support networks and live a better social life
* More likely to have healthy bodies and minds
* Live longer
* More successful in job interviews
* Have stronger immune systems
* Are more productive
* Live better at home
* Promoted faster

* Feel more engaged and motivated

* Be more creative

* More resilient to change and challenges

* Experience less stress

Although this isn't a complete list, you will see how important it is for schools and homes to promote happiness. We must ensure that students and their children are capable of leading, being successful, motivated, and engaged.

Our Emotional State Today

A smile doesn't necessarily mean that someone is happy. Robin Williams was a brilliant comedian and actor, who used his humor to make people smile. The news that he had committed suicide shocked the world.

People who struggle internally often don't display it on the outside. Statistics show that many young people struggle to make a living that is worth living. They often don't share their struggles with anyone. They attempt to find the answer themselves.

Although it may seem strange to tell them they are on the right path, it is true. While I don't suggest that you should struggle on your own, and not seek out assistance, it is important to realize that you are responsible in managing your happiness. You are in a very precarious situation if you entrust your happiness to others. What happens if the person you trust disappears from your life? Are you able to live happily without them?

Young people are often faced with the problem of not knowing where to find happiness. They lack the happiness skills to put their ideas into practice. They are left with no other options than to confide in others. If they don't feel at ease doing this, it is impossible for them to be happy.

It is shocking to see how many people suffer from depression across all ages. While many people with depression never think of suicide, those with depressive disorders are more likely to consider suicide.

According to the Canadian Mental Health Association website almost one-fourth of all deaths in Canada among 15- to 24-year-olds are due to suicide. Suicide is responsible for 16% of all deaths in Canada among adults aged between 25 and 44 years. These are stats we cannot afford to ignore.

Let me add a few facts from the same source:

* Suicide is the second leading cause of death in Canada for 15-24 year-olds (second only to accidents). Each year, 4,000 suicide victims die from premature deaths.

* An alarming 3.2 million Canadians aged 12 to 19 are at high risk of developing depression

* An estimated 10-20% of Canadian youths suffer from a mental disorder or illness - the most severe group of disorders in the world.

* Suicide is a leading cause of death in both men and women, from adolescence through middle age.

* The suicide rate for men is four times higher than that of women

* Today, approximately 5% and 12% of male youths aged 12 to 19 have had a major depressive episode.

* Mental disorders in youths rank second in Canada in hospital care spending, only behind injuries

* Only 20% of Canadian children who require mental health services are provided for by the government.

* About 8% of adults will experience severe depression at one time or another in their lives.

* 20% of Canadians will experience a mental disorder in their lifetime.

Nearly half (49%) people who believe they have suffered from anxiety or depression have never seen a doctor. The situation is worse in Britain and the United States.

According to Young Minds, a UK charity:

26 percent of young people in the UK have suicidal thoughts.

* Teenagers' rates of anxiety and depression have increased by 70% over the past 25 years, especially since the 1980's.

* 55% of bullied children develop depression as adults

These figures are listed on the Jason Foundation website for youth suicide statistics in America:

* Suicide is the second most common cause of death among young people between ten and twenty-four years old

* Suicide is a leading cause of death for teenagers and young adults. This includes heart disease, cancer, AIDS, birth defects and stroke.

* Every day, the USA sees an average of 5,240 suicide attempts per year by students in grades 7-12.

* Fourteens who attempted suicide were among the five that displayed obvious warning signs.

When so many youths are struggling with unhappiness and anxiety, it is hard not to be concerned about them. It is difficult to find positive things to do if you have never been taught happiness skills. Add to that the stigma of mental illness, and it is easy to see why we are failing to help our children, teens, and young adults.

My Happiness Story

This book is written for me personally. I also work with schools and parent groups to increase the mental well-being of our youth. You might be interested in what led me to where you are today. If you don't want to be one of these people, skip this section. I promise not hold it against anyone, nor give away any important information you might regret.

For the first 30 years of my adult life, I was very happy. It doesn't necessarily mean that my life was perfect. Although I had my ups and downs, I knew that all would be well in the end. It has always worked out so far. This belief enabled me to travel to new places and to try new things with a certain amount of confidence.

In passing, I believe that whatever happens in life will be a positive thing, even though I don't understand it immediately. This principle will be discussed in more detail in the precepts.

After six years of teaching in British Columbia, I applied for the commonwealth teaching program. They arrange for you to exchange homes and jobs for one year if they can find a teacher from another commonwealth nation that is suitable for your classes.

I was matched with an English teacher, so I embarked on a 12-month adventure. I knew I would have an incredible time and return home feeling better than I had ever seen.

At the end of my year spent in the UK, I met an Englishman and fell madly for him. Good news! I fell in love. The bad news? The bad news.
Although it was a moment of madness at times, we realized that the best thing for our relationship was to make it more permanent. We were engaged 10 weeks after our first meeting. Before the year was out, we were married.

We made the decision to establish a home in England. It seemed logical because I had spent one year there and enjoyed it. Although I would not be in the same area of the country as London, how could they be so different?

As usual, I was confident in my decision. I had seen it all work out in the past so why shouldn't this? With the hope of living happily ever after, I set my sights on the new adventure.

Although things started off well, I realized that my new life was beginning to take its toll. It was quite different living in a small, rural village in central England to the bustling, lively city of London. In the meantime, I worked full-time in a clothing shop while I tried to get my teaching credentials approved. It was a temporary job that I needed to get by until I could become a teacher.

It is hard to express how much I miss my teaching career. My husband was starting a new job, and I had an exciting life full of friends and social events. Many of these events were shared by my husband, but they weren't my friends or colleagues and I felt totally out of place.

It was hard to keep in touch with family and friends. The internet was still in its infancy, and calls to other countries were costly.

Although it didn't happen in a day, it was a gradual process. However, as the years went by, I found myself in utter despair. My family is prone to mood disorders. Although I thought I had escaped the curse of my family, it wasn't true. After several years of living in my new life, the face I saw in the mirror was no longer the one that I recognized. Although I didn't know what was going on, I knew that I wasn't happy and my life seemed to be getting worse by the day.

It can be difficult to recognize that someone is suffering from mental illness, as I said earlier. It might be hard for you to believe I have depression if you were there when I was a teenager. From a young age, I realized that smiling and laughing was my best way to survive. I was a great actress. Even though I was dying, I could still smile.

For several months, I was constantly sick from one or more illnesses. After seeing my doctor five times in a few months, he identified the root cause of my illnesses.

My husband and in-laws found out that my doctor had prescribed anti-depressants to me because they believed I was depressed. They advised me to keep this information private and to stop taking the medication. They were concerned about side effects and the possibility that I would be viewed as crazy by people if I told them I was depressed. It was and is still widely misunderstood that mental illness is a serious condition. They had the best intentions, but they only made me feel ashamed about what I was going through. I took the medication for one month, but I kept my struggles private. I was not strong enough to question whether or not this decision was right.

I was convinced that my life was not worth living, and that no one would notice if it was over. I spent my time pondering the best way to end it all. This was the place I found myself when I learned that I was actually pregnant.

It was divine intervention. I think it was because I found out I was pregnant. I knew I had to get out of the pit for my unborn child. I was not happy dancing, but I got there.

Awareness is the first step in transformation. I didn't know how I would go from being battered to balanced but I was determined to find a solution. It was hard to find what made me happy, and I didn't know how to get it back.

Looking back at those happy years of my life, it dawns on me that my family and my friends had assumed responsibility for my happiness. I didn't even realize it. They were no longer able to help me when I was married and I moved away. Without saying anything, they believed that my husband would take care of it.

My wonderful husband was not brought up to obey the same rules as my family. He did, however, choose to make me happy and did not consciously decline to do so.

I was following the example set by my parents and looking to my husband for happiness. It was frustrating that he couldn't bring happiness to my life and make it better. This caused a lot of stress in our relationship. It's fair to say I struggled for the majority of the next 20 years to get out of my emotional bind.

I was not just looking for a better place for myself; I also wanted to make sure my children weren't in the same situation.

Now I see that, despite being loved and cared for by my parents, I wasn't equipped with the knowledge and skills to be a happy and healthy child. I was not emotionally prepared to face difficult situations and challenges. My happiness was fragile and it was shattered by changes in my life.

My unhappy life was caused by the person I thought was the problem. He ended up being the one who saved my life. My husband forced me to accept responsibility for my mental health. Without him, I could have been emotionally dependent upon other people my whole life.

I started to research what science had to say about happiness, and found that only I could make myself happy. I was empowered to control my destiny and became stronger. My mother's strategy had left me very vulnerable, so I set out to create a better strategy for my kids.

I began to learn more about positivity and I started to implement them into my parenting. I also shared my knowledge with my children. I made a resolution to do all I could to help them live happier lives than I had.

My son and daughter have become adults who are able to take responsibility for their happiness. However, this doesn't mean you should always look out for yourself and others. Instead of waiting for fate to give you a hand, I encourage you take control and make choices.

Statistics show that it is very common to feel helpless and hopeless. This shows how important it is for young people to learn happiness skills, giving them the understandings and attitudes necessary to be strongly happy.

Section II -
Science Behind the Precepts

Brain Basics

If you want to make the most of your brain's power, it is essential to know a bit about its workings. It can help you to stay focused and not give up when you are learning new skills or trying difficult things. You will also feel more confident to make decisions that will lead you to greater happiness.

Brain Anatomy

The cerebrum, cerebellum and medulla are the three main parts of the brain.

The cerebrum (or cerebral cortex) makes up approximately 85% of brain weight. It is made up of tightly packed nerve cells, called neurons, and it accounts for about 85%. It is the wrinkled outer part of the brain that most people imagine. Higher-level processes such as decision-making and reasoning, memory, language, and reasoning are all controlled by the cerebrum.

The cerebellum, located below the cerebrum, is found at the back of your brain. It is vital for balance and movement, as well as performing voluntary tasks.

The brain stem is also known by the medulla, which is the oldest and most important part of the brain. It is responsible for involuntary functions such as breathing, blinking and digestion. All these are things that our bodies do without conscious thought. The medulla can be found in the middle of the cerebellum and under the cerebrum. It connects the brain and the spinal cord.

Neuroscience 101

The nerve system's specialized cells are neuronal. The neuron is composed of a cell body, dendrites and an axon. The dendrites are able to receive signals from other neurons. The cell body processes the signals and then the axon transmits them out to other neurons. The length of an axon is almost one metre.

About 100 billion neurons make up the brain, which is part of the nervous systems. Each neuron fires approximately 200 times per second and connects with about 1000 others. The neuron sends messages through electrical impulses via their axons and then receives them via their dendrites. It's like a one-way system.

Each activity that the brain orchestrates requires a different set of neurons. Different patterns of brain activity are used for different activities, such as listening, reading, speaking, or thinking. Each activity that we do repeatedly requires our brains to create unique skill patterns.

Gray matter is the cell body. Some people refer to their brains as gray matter. Hercule Poirot, a fictional Belgian detective, refers to his brain as "his little gray cells". However, there are also a lot white matter. Myelin is a fatty white tissue which covers some of the axons in your brain. It makes up almost half of your brain.

Myelination is the process of wrapping myelin around certain parts of the axons. It's designed to improve the speed and strength of electrical impulses. Instead of traveling in a straight line along the axons impulses are forced jump the myelin from one spot to another. Jumping is an easier way for impulses travel.

Myelination occurs naturally in childhood when the brain absorbs every idea and skill that it encounters. Myelination takes longer to develop in adult brains and is more difficult, but it still happens.

How the Brain Learns

The human brain is wired to learn intuitively by watching, experiencing, and then practicing. You will get better at learning the skills you have learned by repeating them over and over. Although new skills might feel awkward or unnatural at first, you will find that they become easier to master and less time-consuming as you practice them. Learning creates new neural pathways.

Every action, thought, and feeling you have comes from impulses that travel from one neuronal cell to the next. Every skill, experience or thought requires a different set of neurons to fire. The stronger the connections between neurons, the more you repeat a pattern.

The brain stimulates the same neural pattern when you repeat an experience or practice a skill. This strengthens their connection. Their connection will be strengthened and they are more likely to fire together in future. Donald Hebb, a Canadian psychologist, stated that neurons that fire together will be more likely to fire together in the future. Conversely, if you stop using a particular skill, your brain may eventually eliminate or prune the connections between these neurons.

Scientists believed that our brains were only capable of learning new things when we are young. This was many years ago. Scientists believed that our brains no longer had the ability to create new patterns once we reach adulthood. Recent discoveries in neuroplasticity prove that this is not true.

Research shows that your brain can learn throughout your entire life. However, you might need to put in a lot more effort than you did when younger. Learning new skills and continuing to improve your existing skills are key to success. It is a wise expression to say, "Use it or Lose it.".

Research has shown that certain regions of the adult brain are just as flexible as those of infants and can still develop. You can build and strengthen connections throughout your life as a lifelong learner. Plasticity allows the adult brain to change its physical structure in much the same way as a child's.

Perfection comes from Perfect Practice

Spend time correcting a skill. It doesn't matter how many baskets you shoot if you don't succeed. You need to pay attention to the quality of your practice and not just the number of repetitions if you want to improve the myelin content in your brain.

You won't be able to master a skill if you don't practice it well. You can improve your skill by practicing often and evaluating your skills. To ensure you are performing the skill correctly, seek feedback if possible. If you practice it correctly, practice will make perfect.

This knowledge can have an impact on homework. Students should not be asked to practice a skill at their home unless they have a method that is reliable and can either evaluate the work they do or provide support. Ineffective practice is not conducive to learning and it's not a good use for time.

Watch this Space

Neuroscience research is growing at an alarming rate. There are new discoveries being made every day, so it is vital to keep up with the latest research. Neurogenesis is a key area in our knowledge of the brain.

Neurogenesis is the term that describes the growth and development neurons.

Scientists believed brain cells were meant to last a lifetime and that once they reached adulthood, they would cease creating new ones. Scientists demonstrated adult neurogenesis in primates and humans in the 1990s. This discovery is likely to have profound implications for neurobiology's future and could lead to new knowledge about the brain's ability learn.

The Importance of Emotions

It's easy to get lost in the pursuit for happiness and believe that there is a perfect life. But that's not reality. Humans would soon be on the slippery slope to their own demise.

Emotions were developed to aid survival in primitive times when humans had to compete with predators and their environment. While the threats that humans see today might not be as severe as those they faced when they were roaming the Savannah with sabre-tooth Tigers, your emotions are still helping you.

Negative Emotions

It is easier to understand the reason for negative emotions. You want to manage negative emotions in a healthy manner, not eliminate them.

Before my Toastmasters group started, I was still sitting in my car. It was already 6.30 am and the light was just starting to shine in the sky. That day, I was giving a speech. Although I enjoy presenting, I was extremely busy that week and had to write my speech before I went to bed. I wasn't sure I would be able to remember everything so I did a final private run-through before I drove off.

I was completely absorbed in my task, when someone knocked on my window. I opened my mouth and gave a quick shout. The smiling face looked in at me then, and I glared back. My expression instantly changed to a smile when I saw who it was.

I lowered the window and held my heart rate steady. Ken, my friend, informed me that he was close to giving me a heart attack.

You may believe that negative emotions are bad and should be avoided because of the media hype surrounding happiness. It is impossible to be more wrong.

Negative emotions are vital for growth and survival. They can raise your alarm and prepare you for a fight or flight response. It's similar to a burglar alarm going off at a bank when someone enters the vault. The bank staff responds immediately to the alarm and does everything they can to protect their customers and bank resources.

Your brain reacts to threats by becoming more aware of the world around it and preparing to defend itself. This is called the fight-or flight response.

Your brain will instinctively choose to stay and face the threat or flee to escape the danger. You rarely choose which one of these responses to follow. The decision is almost always made subconsciously.

This survival mode can cause a variety of things. Your bloodstream is filled with chemicals like cortisol and adrenaline. You become more aware of your surroundings, your vision sharpens, your impulses speed up, and you feel less pain. Your body prepares to face danger or run from it.

This primitive survival response is still there, even if you don't live in the savannah or are threatened by sabre-toothed tigers. Your brain and body still respond to threats when they perceive them.

Your brain will feel most threatened in today's society if it is placed in a win-lose scenario. This could happen when you have a verbal dispute or are preparing to speak to your parent, teacher, or boss.

You will turn to negative emotions if you believe there is only one winner in the conversation. In primitive times, winning meant survival.

In another way, negative emotions can prepare you for battle. Research has shown that if you have a negative outlook, it can make it difficult to gauge your skill level. Conversely, when you feel positive emotions, your skill level is more accurately assessed. It makes perfect sense to understand that your survival is dependent on negative emotions. This allows you to be accurate when assessing your skill-level in times of threat.

Imagine yourself in a fight or flight situation. You might be out on the savanna gathering food when you see a hyena as large as a bear. Is it better to know that you can't outrun it or to tell yourself that you are the best runner in the community so that you can escape to safety with your tribe before he captures you? Precisely! You need to be able to identify the actual skills that you actually have, and not only what you wish you had.

Since primitive times, your reaction to threats has not changed. Although losing doesn't always mean death in modern times, you still feel the need to win.

Ken knocked on my car's window and startedling me. I instantly went into a fight or flight response. My negative emotions were trying to help me defeat my attacker. I quickly realized I wasn't being threatened. I felt my negative emotions lift. However, hormones had released into my bloodstream and my heart rate was racing. My muscles were ready to strike out or run.

My experience is something that almost everyone can relate too. Sometimes we are able to recover quickly and sometimes not as quickly. One time, a friend of mine ran at someone to scare them. He was punched in the face. My friend claimed that his attacker didn't have a sense of humor. In reality, however, the young man acting instinctually was what my friend was referring to.

You may be reverting to a negative outlook if you notice yourself in a losing mindset. Negativity can increase your chances of winning.

Next time you feel a negative emotion, take a moment to notice what your brain is seeing. Accepting that negative emotions are part and parcel of the fight-or-flight response can help you to deal with them positively. It might be easier to empathize and understand others who are in a negative mental state.

The Fight-or-Flight Response in Today's World

Although many of the risks that you face today aren't threats to your survival or health, your brain reacts to them like they are. It's not appropriate to punch or run away from someone you are having a conversation. The best way to behave is to listen and respond calmly and maturely. If your body sends you hormones and more oxygen to allow you to fight or flee, this can be difficult.

Today's world is not conducive to fighting or flight. Therefore, it is common to react aggressively to what is being said.

Imagine a conversation with someone who suddenly became hostile and responded in a dramatic manner. It is possible that you were forced to take a step back in order to see what was wrong.

Do you remember a time in your life when you were hostile to or sensitive to what someone was saying? You might be surprised at your reactions when you think back to the situation. This is how we deal with the fight-or flight response.

It is important to understand what is going on and why. This will help both the person trying to figure out their response and the person being perceived as a threat. In these situations, don't expect to have a calm and rational conversation. Allow the person being threatened to calm down before moving on.

You can help yourself to protect yourself from psychological and not physical threats by paying attention to the signals your body sends you. These signals could be a sign that you are in fight or flight mode. These signals could include muscle tension, heart rate increases, shallow breathing and deep sighing. They can also cause headaches or stomach upsets. These symptoms can also include feelings of anger, fear, hopelessness and poor concentration as well as sadness, sadness, or depression. You can recognize the signs and take action before you become overwhelmed by the threat.

Parents and teachers must recognize and manage their own negative emotions and threats. However, they also have a major role in the lives and development of their children. Avoid situations in which you might unintentionally push children into a corner. This will help to avoid negative emotions and the resulting response.

Do not expect the other person to be reasonable if the response is already triggered. Don't be too harsh if the person is aggressive. This is a primitive response that is embedded in everyone's behavior. They are doing what nature intended them to do when survival is at risk.

You want to have a conversation that conveys your point and produces a positive outcome. Create a safe space where everyone feels comfortable sharing their feelings.

Positive Emotions

Positive feelings make us happy and many people don't stop to think about where they get them. It would be useful to learn more about positive emotions now that we have a better understanding of negative emotions.

Martin Seligman believes positive emotions can trigger a "Here be Growth" mindset. This is the time to be open to learning new skills and making new connections.

Positive feelings can help you see yourself as part of a win-win situation. It is not necessary to fight for survival. This is a time for cooperation and not competition. You are more likely to make new friends and build lasting relationships if you feel good emotions. You are more open to new ideas, more tolerant, and more open to learning. People like you more if you're in a positive mood.

As I said, positivity can make it easy to underestimate your skill-levels. This is called a positivity bias. This helps you take chances, try new things, and make new connections. These are all essential skills for growth.

My school was filled with kids who tried to avoid physical education all their lives. I loved that I wasn't forced to take part in any sporting activities after high school. My dislike of sports didn't stem from an inability to exercise or fear of being seen in shorts at the gym. It was because I felt I had no skills for any sport. I could not throw, catch, or hit a ball more than a few inches with a hockey stick. I was basically useless in any sport that I tried.

In my mid-twenties, while I was out socializing with friends, someone approached me about joining their slow-pitch softball league. I was a regular participant in aerobics and was quite fit. My memory was not accurate and I wasn't as good at throwing and catching as I thought. When I was in highschool, I was worried about embarrassing myself. I felt fine now that I was older.

It is important that you understand that I was in a social setting when the request was made. I was having fun with friends and feeling positive about my life. I was able to agree with them for a reason I didn't fully understand until I learned more about emotions. I'm shaking my head as I read these sentences again. Was that what I was thinking?

What made me change my mind about sports and believe that I had discovered a natural talent that was just waiting to be discovered? Positive feelings made me feel confident, optimistic, and willing to try new things.

Positive feelings can help you believe you are more than you actually are. This confidence boost will make you more inclined to do new things and be bold in social interactions.

Barbara Fredrickson's paper about the function of positive emotions suggests that optimism can help you learn new skills, increase your intellectual and social resources, and even improve your physical and mental health. These skills are available to you when you feel threatened or need them to survive.

Did I find a secret ability to play softball in my past? No! No! The team tried me in several positions before deciding that I should be the back catcher. The first baseman would catch the ball if anyone was running towards Homeplate. To this day, I still find it embarrassing that I allowed every pitch to pass me. I had to run to retrieve it and then give it to the pitcher, who had walked over from home plate because there was no chance that I could throw it to him.

My positive emotions helped me to be brave and try new things. But the first ball that I missed brought back my insecurity and negative emotions. These emotions allowed me to evaluate my abilities and prevented me from developing the mindset I needed to master slow-pitch.

Was I able to persevere? No! After only a few practices and one match, I quit the team. My optimism was fading and I found myself back in the same old mindset and behaviors when it came sports. My negative emotions and my mental outlook led me to believe that I was born without any sporting abilities and that I could not change that.

Emotional Contagion

Emotional contagion refers to the phenomenon where the emotions of one person can cause similar emotions and behavior in others. You may have witnessed this phenomenon in action if you've ever worked with someone who is always negative and complains. Before you know what, everyone is feeling unhappy and disgruntled in the office. Research has shown that positive and negative emotions can spread like a supervirus between people.

Certain people are more prone than others to picking up on the moods of those around them. These people are more likely than others to experience rapid changes in their emotions when they interact with other social groups.

Research has shown that people are more likely to be infected by negative emotions than positive ones. This may be because they react more strongly to bad things that to good. While survival was vital in primitive times, both finding food and avoiding predators was crucial. However, for most people, the need to flee danger was more important than the need for food. While you could miss one or two meals, it was impossible to avoid being caught by a predator. We might not be here if humans were more drawn to food than to danger.

When you realize that you are causing someone's negativity, you can try to distance yourself from them or counteract their negative emotions by trying to be positive. Try smiling or saying something positive for every negative comment they make.

It is important to be aware that you may have a negative effect on others' moods. This can give you a reason to improve your mood, or allow others some space until the negative emotions subside.

Understanding Emotions

Positive and negative moods are necessary in life. While the bad times can make it easier for you to appreciate the positive ones, the good times will prepare you with connections and skills that you can use in times of need. You must have both types of emotions in order to live a fulfilling life.

Learning is best done in a secure and safe environment. This applies to both home and school settings. Cognitive understanding is not fully developed until emotional responses occur. When threatened, you react without thinking. This understanding is essential when you interact with other people.

If you feel threatened, your instincts will make it easy for you to stay with what you know and stop you from learning new skills. It is crucial that parents and teachers create safe and accepting environments in their homes, schools, and classrooms so that everyone feels safe and secure. This requires energy, determination, as well as conscious effort. Section three contains strategies and suggestions for how to accomplish this. Make sure to read the rest of the article.

Perception

I had once upset my husband in the beginning of our marriage and I tried to apologize, but was told I didn't mean it. It was true that I meant it and I felt it necessary to apologize to him. The argument ended in a long, futile struggle that did not result in anything.

It isn't a common occurrence. I have been in this situation both as a receiver and giver. This is an example of perception. Although I truly regret what I said, my husband believes that I just spoke it without any real feeling of regret.

It is always fun to watch my parents share a childhood memory. My mother will often correct him for mistakes in the story that my father tells. My dad then asks my mother if my father was present at the event. He doesn't remember the story she is telling.

This is not a rare situation. The way you see an event can be very different to the way someone else perceives it. You have a powder keg that is ready to go.

Perception refers to the way you interpret non-verbal and verbal signals from others. Your perception of a situation may differ from theirs. My husband may interpret what I say as being unnecessarily aggressive. I, on the other hand, speak in a conversational tone. In situations like this, who is right? Your perception will determine the answer. It's similar to the concept of'subjective wellbeing'. Everybody has their own interpretation.

Positive psychology is all about subjective emotions and perception. The way a person perceives the situation and the emotions associated with it is what will impact them. It may be a concern that your son isn't close enough to his friends. But if he thinks he does, then it's okay. It is his perception that matters. You will reap the benefits of friendships if you believe you have them. It doesn't matter how others think.

You must keep the concept of perception at the forefront of your thoughts when you model happiness. If someone believes you are unfair, they will feel that emotion and they need to deal. It doesn't matter whether you agree or disagree with them.

Communication problems and arguments often stem from differences in perception. Be open to communication and willing to listen even if they aren't your opinion. It's a great way to start moving forward, by valuing the feelings of others.

Hedonic Adaptation

I was a teenager when I attended a weekend conference held in Prince George, British Columbia. One of the main industries there is pulp and paper. After nine hours of driving, I was ready to arrive at our destination. The smell was my first impression as I got out of the car. I was only sixteen years old and my tolerance wasn't set. I would have happily driven nine hours more to get away from the smell, but I didn't want to do that. I was not offered any, so my only option was to try and breathe through my mouth and hope the time flew by.

As the weekend went on, I lost the ability to breath through my mouth and began to be less concerned about the smell. It wasn't until I was ready to go that it occurred to me that I no longer noticed the smell. Even after taking a deep inhale, the odor was still there. It had been unbearable just a few days before.

This story should not deter you to visit Prince George. A few years back, I visited Prince George for work and was struck by the strange smell. The situation has been greatly improved by the addition of mills.

This is a great example of how humans adapt to new situations. Imagine jumping into a pool or lake. Although your first reaction may be to the cold water, you will soon get used to it if you remain in the water for a while.

Not only do you adapt to your physical environment, but also to your emotional one.

Brickman, Coates, and Janoff-Bulman did a study to determine how lottery winners perceived their happiness levels before and after winning. After experiencing an initial surge of happiness, lottery winners returned to the pre-winning levels of happiness.

Numerous studies have been done to investigate the concept of hedonic adaption. There is a range of happiness you can experience, regardless of your emotional highs or lows. You will always return to that range of happiness. It is similar to the thermostat in your home. The temperature control controls the furnace and air conditioners to maintain the right temperature as the air cools or heats up.

In the section about the importance of emotions, I introduced Martin Seligman's phrase "Here be Growth" to describe how you feel when you experience positive emotions. He used the opposite term to describe negative emotions, 'Here are dragons. Let me add another term to the mix. This is what I call 'Here Be Complacency'. It can be used to describe extreme happiness. This is what you might feel when you first find out that you're a millionaire. You may feel like this when you get married, get the promotion you have been trying for five years or any other situation that makes you happy. You stop feeling the need to improve and grow when you're at this level of happiness. It's easy to just enjoy the feeling and not move.

Think about these three states. Feeling negative emotions because of perceived danger, feeling positive, ready to learn, or feeling happy and content and enjoying the moment. Which of these states is best for you?

Experts agree that the growth state is what you would call it. You wouldn't learn, grow, or progress if you got good news but then spent the rest of your life in a state that euphoria. You wouldn't be in a position to sustain your survival. You would also not be able to grow and move forward if you were always in a negative, unproductive state, such as being stuck down, preparing for danger.

You should be in a moderately to moderately happy state. This is where you feel confident, open to new experiences and ready to make connections. Hedonic Adaptation will pull you down when your happiness becomes so great that you lose sight of the real world. Then, it will come in like a super-hero and pull you up when your life is going sour. This is why life can be so unpredictable. This is a normal cycle that everyone experiences. It's not something you should be ashamed of.

Don't feel sad if you begin to notice that your extreme happiness is gone. Your brain is responsible for your survival. You can rest assured that your brain will adapt to any situation, even if it is difficult.

Your Equation for Happiness G + C + IA = H

Happiness = Genetics + Circumstance + Intentional Activities

Research has shown that genetics, circumstances and intentional activity are the factors that determine your level of happiness. Happiness is not a single point. It is a collection of normal feelings for you.

Genetics

All traits inherited from your parents are genetics. 50% of your mother's genes and 50% from you biological father.

Neurotransmitters are brain chemicals that transmit messages between neurons and affect your emotions. Your genetic code determines how you brain uses these chemicals. This is one area where nature has the ability to give you a hand, or make it difficult.

Circumstance

Your environment is how you interact with it. This includes your family, financial situation, and profession.

Intentional activity

Intentional activity is defined as something you consider and make a conscious decision about. Intentional activity is a way to react to the circumstances that arise without your input.

Nature vs Nurture

You can be happy by your genes, your nature, and the way you were raised. But which is more important? Is it your genes or the person who raised you that holds the key to your happiness?

For decades, the debate has raged over who controls us more: nature or nurture. It is difficult to separate genetics and environmental influences. It is hard to discern between genes and environmental influences in life.

Your happiness is likely to be affected more by your circumstances if you worry about your ability to pay rent or buy food.

You may not inherit all the traits you have. While you may be predisposed to risky behavior, depression, and alcoholism, that does not mean you will become alcoholic or clinically depressed. The gene could remain silently in your background for the rest of your life if the environment that set it into motion doesn't happen.

It is therefore difficult to determine how much of your wellbeing is affected by nature and how much is caused by nurture. It's impossible to separate the two. The environment can either turn genetic traits on and off or make them dormant. Both factors can have a significant impact on your life satisfaction.

David Lykken, Auke Tellegen and others have studied over 1,300 pairs of twins to determine the contribution of genetics to happiness levels. The studies covered identical and non-identical twins of the same sex. The study looked at twins who were raised together as well as those who were separated at birth, and who were raised in different environments.

The studies revealed that the circumstances and life events of identical twins did not make a difference when compared to their counterparts. Even though they were raised separately from each other, identical twins had very similar levels of happiness. Even if one of the twins was assessed at twenty-five and the other at thirty, this was still the case. This means that even if identical twins were raised in completely different environments, they would still experience the same level of happiness. This is a strong indicator that your life satisfaction may be genetic.

Not all Variables are Equal

Please forgive me if mathematicians are reading this. Because not all variables have the same weighting, it is inaccurate. This is how the equation should look:

G * 5 + C + IA * 4 = H

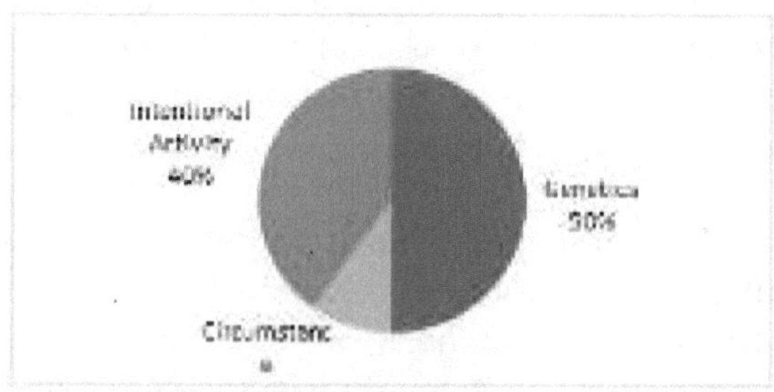

Let's make the equation more clear by making it a pie chart.

The graph shows that scientists believe up to half of your happiness is due to your genes, 10% to your circumstances, and 40% to intentional activity.

This information will help you dispel the myth that improving your situation will bring long-term happiness. It doesn't really matter what you do, it won't make a difference how happy you are over a long period of time.

You can think back to Hedonic Adaptation. You will only feel temporarily affected by circumstances that cause your happiness to soar. Then your mood will return to normal. You will not be able to achieve a long-term happiness level by changing your circumstances.

However, you can change your happiness level significantly, regardless of your genes and your circumstances if your focus is on intentional activity. This is the only variable you can control and is responsible for at most 40% of your positive emotions.

You cannot control the circumstances that lead to a school surprise test. You decide what you do in this situation. You have two options: complain about the unfairness of the teacher or you can accept your results and learn from the mistakes so that you're ready for the next exam.

Positive thinking activities can increase your happiness levels. These activities include setting goals, being kind to others, surround yourself with positive people and taking care of your physical, mental, and social well-being.

Motivation

I believed I had all the necessary skills to be a good teacher when I began teaching elementary school. I didn't know what it meant to make me feel needed. I vividly recall a social studies lesson at the end of school. I was looking up and saw that everyone was completely absorbed in their work. As students from different stations worked together, there was a great buzz. They discussed how to best complete the tasks.

I can remember thinking, "What do I do now?" They don't even need me!" It was strange to feel this way, as I hadn't thought of my role as a teacher that involved creating independent students. Although I was initially concerned by the discovery, I soon realized that my goal was to help children become more engaged in their education.

Nothing is more satisfying than seeing someone completely engaged in learning or practicing a new skill. While some people naturally exhibit this behavior, others struggle to find the time and are unable to focus on learning new skills and knowledge.

Science can provide useful information that will help you create an environment where students are encouraged to learn. You can avoid discipline problems in your classroom by motivating your students. A lack of belief or interest can often lead to bad behavior.

Psychologists believed there were two main reasons why people are motivated: incentive-driven and biological. We eat because of our hunger (biological), and we study hard to get good grades in school (incentive).

Harry F. Harlow, a professor of psychology from the University of Wisconsin, began an experiment in learning in 1949. Eight rhesus monkeys were involved in the research. He created a simple mechanical puzzle to prepare them for the study. To see how they respond, Harlow placed several in monkey cages. Harlow was shocked to discover that the monkeys started to play with the puzzles without any encouragement. Harlow was even more surprised to see that the monkeys seemed to enjoy the activity.

They quickly solved the problem and were able to do it again.

... and more. This was not compatible with any of the previously identified motivations. The monkeys did not have a biological need to solve the puzzles and they were not being given any incentives. Harlow was surprised by this behavior and suggested an intrinsic reward as a reason for motivation. The monkeys solved the puzzles because they received positive feelings and enjoyed the process.

You have likely learned about intrinsic and extrinsic motivation if you have taken psychology courses. External motivation, also known as extrinsic or intrinsic, is motivated by external factors such as rewards, evaluations and bonuses. It can be either positive or negative. It could be to get good grades (positive) or to avoid being lectured by your parents (negative). These are both examples of intrinsic motivators. Intrinsic motivation is internal motivation. It's the desire to do something that makes you happy or makes someone else happy.

The Self-determination Theory

Edward Deci was a psychology graduate student at the time and began looking for a topic for his dissertation. After stumbling upon Harlow's research, Deci became intrigued in continuing it. Richard Ryan joined Deci and they developed the self-determination theory. This model suggests that you must satisfy three human needs in order to feel motivated: autonomy, competence, and relatedness.

Competence means believing you can do something well enough to succeed; autonomy is the belief you have some control over what you do; and relatedness refers to feeling that you are connected with others. Your students and children should feel motivated to school if they are confident in their ability to learn, feel that they have some control over school, and feel connected to the school.

It's important to remember that the child's perception will determine whether or not any of these needs are satisfied. The child must feel they have the ability, autonomy, and connectedness to satisfy their need. If you have not read the section about perception, I recommend it. It is an important aspect of the discussion on human behavior.

You, as a parent or teacher, need to communicate with students and families to understand their perspectives. It is not enough to create autonomy for others and assume that they have satisfied their needs. Your student may not believe that they are competent, autonomous, or related. The power of the self determination theory is entirely dependent on perception.

A Warning about Incentives

We live in an age of incentives. We believe that children will succeed if they are rewarded for good grades, and that employees will be more productive if they get a bonus. Harlow's research revealed a new kind of motivation. The research also revealed interesting information about incentives.

Harlow believed that motivations or biological needs were more important than internal motivations, so he withheld food from the monkeys for twenty-two hours. Then he showed the hungry monkeys that he was feeding them by placing food in the puzzles and then putting them in their cages. The monkeys thought they would quickly open their familiar puzzles to get to the food, but instead of solving the puzzles as they have done many times before, they made even more mistakes. After the puzzles had been opened and the food was eaten, the monkeys lost interest in them. It was apparent that the puzzles no longer hold the same enjoyment.

Harlow's motivation research was not well received by the scientific community, so he moved on to other areas of his work. Deci discovered it later and was fascinated, eager to develop the discoveries Harlow made.

Deci designed a study with college students and Soma Cubes (a puzzle that has pieces that can be glued together to create different shapes). Students were split into two groups. Participation in the study required that students come to the lab three times, and then repeat the process again. Participants were given magazines and soma cubes each time they arrived at the lab.

All students received the same treatment during their first visit. The students were shown a picture and asked to create the puzzle shapes themselves. Deci instructed the students to complete several shapes and told them that they needed to log their progress into the computer. They could also do anything they wanted while he was gone.

It was common in 1968 to leave the room in order to enter the results into the computer. Computers at the time were large enough that they could occupy an entire space. Deci didn't intend to enter the results into a computer. He instead went to the next room and observed the activities of the student during his free time.

When all students were treated the exact same way during their first visit, they preferred to continue playing with the puzzle. They enjoyed creating new shapes. This behavior was observed for students in group B. They participated with no expectation of rewards.

On the second visit, group A members were informed that they would be paid for every shape they created. They worked on the puzzles in their spare time to make more money. This is in line with common beliefs about the power of incentives.

On the third visit to the lab by members of group A, they were informed that there was no money and that they would not receive any payment for the shapes they created in that session. These students lost interest in puzzles and began to read magazines when they learned this. The members of group A, on the other hand, continued to enjoy the puzzles throughout the three sessions. They were still interested in them.

Deci concluded that incentives were not only short-term solutions but could also be detrimental to internal motivation. Similar results were found in other studies. It seems that humans are programmed to believe that if you have been rewarded for doing something, you shouldn't do it just because you like it?

Many parents and professionals in the education and business fields believe that extrinsic rewards are the best way to motivate. Are you aware of any instances where money or other incentives were offered to students for high school grades or outstanding work performance? Research shows that this is not a good idea to encourage engagement and intrinsic motivation.

Don't give your children an allowance that is tied to specific tasks if you don't want them to. It is important to teach your children how to manage money. However, it doesn't matter if they get their work done. You can help your children's internal motivation to help around the house by not linking chores and money.

The Needed Nine

In his book, Work, Unemployment and Mental Health, Peter Warr introduced the world the 'Needed Nine' features of happiness. These nine features are the main sources of happiness or unhappiness that you can find in any part of your life. These are:

1. Personal influence

   You should feel at least some autonomy and control over what happens to you. Nobody wants to feel micromanaged or be at the mercy the world around them.

2. Using your abilities

   Opportunities to use their skills and to improve are essential for everyone. You don't have to do only what you know, but it is essential to be able to apply your skills to solve problems and achieve goals.

3. Demands and goals

If you want to feel happy, you must be required to perform certain tasks. It's like having a purpose and a reason for getting up each morning. We often set goals for ourselves but research shows that we need the environment to help us achieve our goals.

4. Variety

This is the "spice" of life. Research supports this old saying. It is easy to fall into routines and patterns. However, being stuck in the same place or repeating the same thing over again can lead to negative emotions. The human brain resists repetition.

5. Clear requirements and outlook

Uncertainty about the future and your expectations can lead to anxiety for anyone, even those who take risks. Research repeatedly shows that happiness is hard to achieve if you're not sure what to do or unable to predict what your future holds. Both of these are essential for making sound decisions.

6. Social contacts

Humans are social creatures. Without friendships and interaction, it's difficult to feel happy. A happy school or home is only possible if you are part of a group. These contacts will help you to better understand yourself and gain a greater perspective on the world around.

7. Money

Although this is not something that affects all children, it can affect them if their parents are concerned about how they will pay the bills and provide food for their families. Your happiness will be affected if you don't have enough to provide for your needs. However, those who believe that winning the lottery will make them happy are sadly mistaken. Increased wealth will not make you happier once you have enough money to pay the rent or feed your family. Many wealthy people feel lonely and unfulfilled.

8. Adequate physical setting

Your environment must provide you with safety and security. If they are to foster learning, schools, homes, and classrooms must provide safe havens.

9. A valued role

It is important to feel valued and do something that makes a difference. You can increase your job satisfaction as a teacher by seeing your role as one that guides the next generation of leaders, change-makers, and not just showing up at your classroom to make a buck. The family's happiness will be shared by parents who have a similar view.

The children must also see their work as valuable, either for themselves or for the benefit of others.

Section III - Precepts

Introducing the Precepts of Robust Happiness

This section will discuss the eight precepts that lead to robust happiness. Precepts are principles that can be applied to your life. While knowledge is essential, it won't make you change. If you want to see transformation, you must act on that information.

There is a lot of overlap among the precepts. These precepts are closely linked, so if you include one in your life, you'll find other elements. A single action can encourage you to add several precepts. These precepts can help you create happiness that can withstand challenges and help you stay mentally strong all your life.

It is important to remember that modeling the elements and talking about them openly is the best way to assist others. You will be more successful at inspiring others to live a happy lifestyle if you model it. We can't afford not to address the depressing statistics of mental health organisations around the world.

While your children may appear happy and well-adjusted and that is a good thing, it's important to remember the many silent sufferers. Everybody needs to be able to take control of their happiness. It's up for us all to ensure that children have the information and tools they need to live a life of solid happiness.

Precept #1

Enjoy the Journey

How do you imagine living a happy, fulfilled life? Are you imagining having bad hair days and being frustrated with your family? Most people imagine a world where there are no negative emotions or annoyances. You may think that having a lot of money and the possibility of retiring from your job are top options.

You will see that your emotions are designed to have good and bad times. It's unrealistic to expect happiness every day. To achieve robust happiness, you should experience more positive emotions and less negative ones.

The environment you live in is constantly changing and something that you can't control. It's not the challenges that make us unhappy; it's the way we deal with them. It is exhilarating to face a challenge and triumph over it. These are some of the most rewarding experiences in life.

Our society may promote the notion of never-ending happiness. However, this is not reality. If you believe that it is, you will be disappointed. Chasing happiness can be likened to following a butterfly. As soon as you are close, the butterfly flies off to another plant. Even if you do catch happiness, hedonic adaption (see The Science Behind the Precepts), exists to make sure you return to your desired level of well-being.

Positive feelings can give you the boost you need to get through difficult or new tasks. These emotional highs are great, but they don't last forever. You would not be able to adapt to changes in your environment if you feel ecstatic constantly.

Jason Riis, the lead author, decided to compare happiness levels between healthy people and dialysis patients. For a week, each participant was required to have a Palm Pilot. The devices would vibrate every ninety minutes. Each participant was asked to choose the word when they did.

The most accurate description of how they felt at the moment was happy, joyful, anxious, or unhappy. The results showed that patients with renal disease were as happy as healthy people.

An analysis of breast cancer patients revealed that the majority felt their lives were better within the first month to five years following their surgery. Many people have experienced a complete shift in their outlook on life after a close call with death. These people suddenly realize what is most important and what makes their lives happy. It is rare that retirement dreams have anything to do. Enjoy the moment, as there's no guarantee that the time in the future you want will come.

To create robust happiness, the first principle is to recognize that the joy in life is not in achieving a goal or reaching a destination. It is important to focus. However, if you place so much emphasis on a future event that you miss the opportunities to appreciate what is happening around you, then you will be missing out on many opportunities to experience what is already happening.

George and Laura worked hard their whole adult lives. They decided to save as much as they could to pay for their retirement. Their goal was to do this as soon as possible. They put off going on holidays and enjoying their hard-earned money, all in an effort to improve their lives for the future. They retired at the age they chose and left work smiling and full of anticipation and adventure.

George was diagnosed with early-onset dementia two months after he and Laura started their new lifestyle. His life, which he and Laura had lived for many decades, was suddenly changed from one of joy to one of anxiety.

Practice Consciousness

Did you ever travel home from work only to find that you have lost all your memories of how you got there, or are you still unsure where you were?

This is not uncommon and shows how it's possible to live your life and forget about the people and experiences you have around you.

Have you ever heard people talk about the "little things" that make them happy, or the "last straw" that makes them miserable? Many small things can lead to big things.

There have been many people who were caught off guard by the news that their partner was unhappy and planning to end their relationship. It is possible that they have been unhappy for many years and their partner didn't know. This is what happens when you don't live in the present. Because your eyes are fixed on the future, you don't often notice what's happening around.

Instead of focusing on the future, take the time to appreciate the moment. This is not to suggest that you should avoid the future. While setting goals and dreaming big is important, don't get too rigid about the route you choose. Don't let your dreams distract you from the moment. If you don't miss the moments, you won't be able to get your precious early years back.

Mindfulness is hot and well-researched. You can enjoy all that life has to offer by being fully present. You can increase your happiness by living in the present. Enjoy your day and take the time to appreciate it.

The Serenity Prayer

God, grant me the peace to accept what I can't change.

Courage to make a difference in the world.

Wisdom to be able to tell the difference

Enjoying the journey can be difficult. You have to learn to accept the fact that not all things are within your control. It's a waste to try to change something you can't control. You can't force someone to change their mind, no matter how hard you try. They can't make the decision for you.

Goal Setting

However, you should not solely focus on the future.

It is not something you can ignore. It is important to know where you are going. Imagine you are on holiday and have no idea where it is going to end up. How will you find out when you get there? While I know there are some people who believe spontaneity is the best way to travel, please bear with me. You will need to have some sort of plan if you only have a short time to get home.

Goal setting is a strong indicator of happiness and satisfaction. Research has shown that the key to setting goals is not in achieving them. This is consistent with the idea that joy lies in the journey, not where you end up. It doesn't matter if you set a goal in stone. You can write it in the sand where it is easily modified. However, this doesn't mean you have to set a goal for weight loss and then eat potato chips. You are what makes you happy. It won't help your mood to set goals that you don't intend to work towards.

Goal setting is easier when you view happiness as a journey rather than a destination. Your goals can be viewed as milestones or lights on your journey. Each goal is just the beginning of your adventure. Enjoy your successes and set another goal to continue your journey. Every milestone is a sign that you're moving forward and it helps you believe you can achieve the next goal.

If your journey takes you to a place you didn't intend, don't be discouraged. You will find more happiness when you work towards a goal, than when you achieve it. Unexpected bumps and drops in the road can teach you a lot about yourself and your surroundings. It is important to be able to adapt to unexpected turns in your path.

Maintain a Flexible Approach

It is evolutionary wisdom to be able to adapt and change with your environment, whether you are looking back at your distant ancestors or your current situation.

You need to be flexible in your outlook on life. Things rarely go according to plan. Because your environment and circumstances change constantly, adaptability is essential. You must adapt to the changes in your environment and surroundings in order to survive and thrive. It is impossible to remain static.

It was not something that I was born with. As a child, my parents taught me to be resilient to change. This was how I dealt with unexpected changes as I entered adulthood. Although I am better at adapting with practice, it is something I still need to work on.

Avoid being Judgemental

Growing up, I was raised in a family that valued opinions on the decisions and choices of others. My parents believed that the best way to live life would be for my siblings and me. They could also be negative about decisions we made that were not in our best interests. It can be hard to remain strong when you are faced with resistance. Although I was aware of the choices that my parents believed would be best for me, they weren't always the ones I wanted to make. This is something that many children face as they get older.

As an adult, I have tried to not judge other people's choices. I hope that they will do the same for me. I don't know the details of anyone's journey, nor do I know what I would do if I were living a different lifestyle. Although it is easy to believe you can predict how you will react to a situation, as you get older, I have come to realize that you don't know what you would do if you are in the same situation.

Judging others is one of most destructive acts that you can commit. Consider how you feel when someone judges your decisions. Are you sure they have the right to? This is a difficult skill to master for parents, as you want the best for your kids and think you know more. It doesn't matter if you know more. If we want to be happy, each of us must learn how to navigate our lives. Offer support and advice, but be open to accepting the learning opportunities offered by others.

The Principle

Your brain is programmed to feel a range of emotions throughout your life. You can't always be happy. This knowledge can be used to create a life with more goodness than harm. You will be happy again if you accept challenges and low points. Hedonic adaptation will ensure that you feel happy again.

Each person has their own path to follow. They are the only ones who can truly know the details of each step. You can guide when needed, offer advice when requested, but you don't have to take over someone else's lives with the false belief that they know best.

When things don't go as planned, you learn more. This keeps you flexible and allows you to learn new skills.

Let children fail and learn. Let them fail and learn, but it's not better to have them experience success. For anyone to be strong and happy, they must learn how to handle failure.

Don't judge other people's decisions. Remember that everyone is on their own journey and they must take responsibility for it. It is important to accept that not everyone is the same as you, for your happiness and the happiness of your students and loved ones.

Action

1. Find out the purpose of your emotionsUnderstanding emotions and their purpose can help you increase the enjoyment of your journey. It can be easier to accept the challenges life brings by being aware of your fight-or flight response and hedonic adaption.

2. Live in the moment

Instead of focusing on the future, be mindful of what's happening right now in your life. These strategies will help you to appreciate the moment:

a. Practice meditation
b. Enjoy the sights and sounds around you.
c. Take a look at, draw or photograph your surroundings
d. Keep a diary and reflect on the day. What went well? What are you thankful for? What could you have done differently?

e. Before you get out of bed every morning, make a goal for the day.
    i. You can take a break throughout the day to remember your intention
    ii. Reflect on the day and reflect on how it went.

3. Enjoy the entire journey

You should start the field trip or holiday as soon as your front door opens. You can challenge your companions to discover interesting sights and sounds along the way to your destination.

4. Become a people watcher

Pay attention to the decisions and choices made by others. But don't judge them. Watching the people around us can help you learn a lot.

5. Accept others for who they areYou don't have to like everyone who crosses your path. But, you should allow them the freedom to live their lives and learn their lessons. You don't have to expect everyone else to behave the same way. Model accepting, nonjudgemental behavior.

6. Be resilient when others judge your decisionsBe strong even when you feel judged. Remember the importance of taking control of your own life. You made the best decision based on your current situation. You can learn from it if it doesn't go your way. It will make you richer.

7. Your students and your children will follow you as a guide.Show others how important it is to be responsible for their own lives. Encourage them to see that there are both good and bad times in life, and that they can

learn from those difficult times. Provide comfort and insight, but allow them to make their own decisions.

8. Please share your experiences with othersIt can be very comforting to know that others have gone through similar problems as you. Talking with people who have been through similar situations can be incredibly comforting. It is important to have a healthy conversation about emotions and the challenges that you face. This will allow others to share their feelings and experiences. The old saying "A trouble shared is an opportunity halved" is very true.

9. Create Goals

It is important to be able see the progress you have made on your journey. These goals are not destination or endpoints but markers on your journey. They will increase your positive feelings of wellbeing.

Tips for Creating Goals

1. Set goals that are easily measuredIt can be hard to determine if you are succeeding if you just want to be happier. It is important to know how to assess whether your mood is improving.

2. You can list both long- and short-term goalsBoth goals can contribute to your happiness.

3. Be cautious about who you share your accomplishments and goals withIt may seem insensitive to tell someone who has failed a performance review that they are the employee of the month.

4. Be aware of your responses when others share their goals.A person who shares positive feelings about a person's goals or good news will feel more comfortable if the listener responds with a supportive message and nonverbal cues showing genuine interest and pleasure.

5. Keep an achievement diary

Each day, list your achievements and pick one to reflect upon. Consider how this has impacted your life. You should be proud of the work you did. Although it may take several months to see the positive effects of this activity on your happiness, I promise you that it will be well worth the effort.

6. You can shoot for the stars but don't expect to reach your goals overnight.It's better to believe that the path ahead will require you digging deep, and then to be pleasantly surprised if it doesn’t, rather than believing everything will go smoothly and then being disappointed.

7. Be sure to take the time to review your expectationsYou can try to control your expectations if they seem too high. Instead of feeling disappointed by something that doesn't live up to your expectations and seeing it as a failure instead, consider the lessons learned along the journey.

Conclusion

You will never be happy no matter how successful you are in your life or the journey you take. Both positive and negative emotions will be experienced. Both positive and negative emotions are necessary for personal growth and survival. It is easier to cope with difficult times when you know that your life is meant to include a range of emotions.

Children should be taught from a young age about the meaning of emotions. It is important for children to learn that all feelings have a purpose and are necessary. They will be able to better understand themselves and others.

Find a way that you can enjoy your journey to happiness. This will make you a happier person. Be open to the possibility of others being on a similar journey as you are.

Precept #2

Create a Mindset for Success

> *You can do it, regardless of whether you think so or not.*
>
> Henry Ford

Mindset

Mindsets are a set of beliefs you hold that are important to how you view and evaluate your life.

Carol Dweck's Mindset was a book I came across a few years back. As I had to commute long distances for work, I was looking for an audio book that I could listen to in my car. I was literally transformed by the information I received. The book was both hard and audio, and I purchased the audio version to highlight key sections. This book is a favorite of mine, and I listen to it at least once per year.

Mindset is a must-read book. Dweck discusses fixed and growth mindsets in Mindset, which are two very different views of intelligence and abilities.

Fixed versus Growth

Fixed-minded people believe intelligence is predetermined. They believe you are born with certain abilities that will never change. Geniuses are not born. You can be smart and do most things without any instruction if you're smart.

The foundation of a fixed mindset is natural ability. You will always be smart if you were born smart. It's okay if you don't have natural abilities. This mindset will make you a failure and a success.

This was the mindset that I used for the first three to four decades of my adult life. This fixed mindset also meant that I was able to compare myself with my siblings and found myself lacking. Because I believed I was less gifted than my sister and brother, I avoided challenges and did only what I knew I could succeed at. I didn't want my family or me to be wrong about my intelligence. The feelings I felt about my intelligence weren't a fact, but a suspicion.

My fixed-minded parents believed I was less capable than my siblings. Although I doubt they would admit it, it is possible. My sister was three years old when my brother was born. My mom spent many hours with him during those years. At an early age, he learned to read and scored very well on an IQ test. Keep in mind that one belief of the fixed mindset is predetermined ability. So if my brother was brilliant at five years old, he would continue to be bright throughout his life. My parents were proud as punch.

I was my third child and was very similar in age to my older sibling. My speech was not clear until I was three years old. If I grunted, my older sister would be able to understand me and take over the speaking. My parents viewed me as the social child. I was bright and happy as a child.

Do any of these sound familiar? Are you from a fixed-minded family or were you raised by one?

A growth mindset is better than a fixed mindset. This attitude recognizes that intelligence and abilities you were born with are only a starting point. With effort and learning, you can become smarter. You believe in continuous learning and are open to new opportunities. Failure at a challenge is not a sign that you are a failure. This simply means that you aren't ready to do the activity yet. You might be able to do it the next time if you practice and get more experience.

One can choose to have both of these mindsets or one in each area of your life. While both are valid, a growth mindset is more important if you want happiness.

People with a fixed mindset believe geniuses can be born and do things naturally without effort. This is how they want others to see them. They should be seen as effortless successful. For those who have a fixed mindset, getting A's without ever having to do any homework or trying is a highly desirable quality. You feel pressure to appear smart and naturally talented all the time. This can lead to a lot of stress and a lot of energy wasted trying to maintain that image.

Fixed-minded people are more worried about others thinking they are smart than you. This mindset thinks intelligence is a result of luck. If you don't feel smart right now, it doesn't mean you weren't or won't be. You don't want situations where you might find this surprising thought true, so if you, like me, have a fixed mentality and suspect you lack natural ability, it is best to not be like me.

Fixed-minded students are more focused on appearing smart than learning. Carol Dweck and her colleagues discovered that children with a fixed mindset were more concerned about appearing smart than learning. They often lie about how well they did on activities for another part of their research.

For this reason, I must admit to having lied once.

It was PE 10. We were doing a unit of grass hockey. Our mark was based upon different skills that we should have learned during the unit. One was the ability to drive the hockey puck. The distance you could propel the ball was what determined your letter grade.

I couldn't for the life get the ball beyond a D distance. The teacher allowed those who wanted to improve their scores to have that opportunity, while the rest of class played a game. I couldn't get the hockey ball above the D mark, no matter how hard I tried.

In a moment of defiance I finally went over to the teacher to tell him that I had reached the C marker. I rationalized my behavior by saying that grass hockey was not going to affect my grade point average.

My fixed mentality was telling me I could justifiably justify the things I did, even though it wasn't my best work. I was more concerned about the grade than learning a new skill or getting better at grass hockey.

Students who are trying to prove themselves don't care about what they did wrong on their assignments or tests. They are only interested in the marks they get. School is about appearing intelligent and confident for students with a fixed mindset.

Post-secondary education is often viewed as a memorization exercise by students with a fixed mindset. You should be able to recall enough information from printed materials to be able answer questions correctly. It's not about understanding or learning the material. It's about getting a good mark.

These students believe it is more important for them to be smart than to learn new skills or information. These students avoid taking chances that could lead to what they consider failure. It's better to get a good grade than one you don't have. Students with a fixed outlook will find school all about showing others and themselves that they are intelligent.

When I was at the top, I felt the most pressure to do well in university. I didn't want my success to be questioned. I chose assignments and projects that would keep me on top of my class, over those that would allow me to grow as a teacher, learner, and person. It was more important to receive a high grade than to learn something.

Parents and teachers who have a fixed outlook may be motivated by their need to prove that they are naturally intelligent. Sometimes you may pretend to know the answer or believe you are right all the time. If someone suggests an alternative viewpoint, or that you are wrong, this can often manifest itself in defensive and aggressive behavior.

Fixed-minded parents place emphasis on their children's ability to learn quickly and without instruction. It is a sign that your child is a genius if she learns to read by herself. Children who are not taught how to read or who learn reading at an earlier age are less gifted. They believe that a child who is able to read and write well as a toddler will continue to be able to do the same thing for the rest of his or her life.

Tracy and Don's daughter was now in school and needed to decide which school to send her to. They lived closest to the one with the lowest academic record. Many of the children who attended the school were not from well-off families.

Because they wanted their child to come from a better family, they settled for the local school. They stated that she would rather be a large fish in a small lake than a small fish within a large pond.

Their child excelled in school and was awarded many academic awards. Although their decision was valid, the reasoning behind it is typical of fixed-minded parents. It's better to appear smarter in a group with less educated students than to be average among a group full of geniuses.

It is hard to accept criticism when you have a fixed mindset. You will interpret criticisms of your abilities as a threat to you ability if they point out any flaws. This can lead to a need to justify and deflect. It is not your fault. You are not responsible for the failure to do well.

You will likely recall watching audition hopefuls get furious when they were turned down on reality TV like American Idol. The judges were stupid, the show was rigged, and no one knew what good music meant. These are the perfect examples of people with a fixed mindset. These contestants were more inclined to quit when things got difficult than to persevere and overcome obstacles.

People with the growth mindset are not able to accept these beliefs and behaviors. If they compare their academic careers later on, they believe that someone who has been taught how to read can read as well or better than someone who was self-taught. Although it is possible to be born with natural abilities, this doesn't guarantee success in life or your ability to learn.

Students with a growth mindset understand that school is not about being smart but learning. Adults with this mindset accept the fact that learning takes effort and time, and that it will continue for a lifetime. They don't feel the need for others to have similar abilities. Everyone learns at their own pace, depending on how hard and how often they practice.

This set of beliefs made American Idol contestants more likely to pay attention to the critiques from the judges and to take away the lessons learned. They didn't view the criticisms as malicious or personal, even if they were harsh. Negative evaluations can be used to help you improve. Growth mindset contestants were more likely to put in twice as much effort during the week, even if the feedback was negative.

People with a fixed outlook find it difficult to live without labels. Fear of losing a positive label and fear of being deserving of a negative one are two sides to the same coin. It's easier to quit than to risk losing your top status or showing people that you are worthy of being at the bottom. Good labels are a reflection of your effort and bad labels highlight areas where you can improve. Some people may believe that they are at the bottom, but that if they work hard, they can climb up to the top.

Viewing Failure

Fixed mindsets focus on avoiding making mistakes because they believe that failure is the definition of success. They see the world as a series of win-lose scenarios. As you will recall from previous sections, win-lose situations can cause you to feel negative emotions when you are preparing to flee or fight. Fixed mindsets don't make people as happy as those who have growth mindsets. They see everything in their world as a win-lose situation. They will work hard to avoid any challenges they don't believe they can overcome. They believe that if victory is not certain, it is better to not participate.

You can have fun with what you do even when faced with adversity if you have a growth mindset. A lack of success is not viewed as failure. Instead, it's seen as an opportunity to learn. You should not be afraid to take risks in your life. It is important to appreciate the help of others in order to reach your goals. When times are tough, you don't give up. Instead, you persevere and overcome the problem knowing that you are becoming smarter and building stronger neural pathways.

Enjoying Your Journey

This mindset will help you to have a more enjoyable journey. You don't need to worry about what others think of you if you work hard or fail to reach your goals.

How you live your life will be affected by how you think. Fixed mindsets are designed to preserve your intelligence and to show others how smart you really are. Instead of focusing on learning, focus on proving that you already know.

I have shifted from the rigid mindset that I held in the beginning of my life and have been working hard to create a growth mindset. However, there are times when I slip back into old ways. My belief is that people's true potential lies in their own hands. Although you may have achieved something amazing at an early age, imagine what you can achieve with passion, hard work, and learning. I'm relieved to say that past performance does not determine my future success.

Changing Your Mindset

You can change your mindset, but it is possible. This is because you have already done that. Sometimes, it takes someone else to prove to us that we can learn something we don't know how to do before we believe it is possible.

My fixed mentality led me to believe that I didn't have any athletic abilities. I avoided physical education as much as I could. When I couldn't get out of it, I did my best to avoid the activity. There's no need to prove that I am useless to anyone, even if it was my best effort.

I was married to a family of tennis players. Everyone was competitive and I was worried about how I would fit in. My father-in law taught PE at a youth offenders' institution, and he wasn't convinced that I could be as bad.

To get him to stop harping on me about tennis, I allowed him to teach me. My point was clear after just one visit to the court.

My father-in law is a great tennis coach. My father-in-law is a great tennis coach. He taught me skills that are so simple even I can succeed. For example, he bouncing the ball straight to me so I could catch it. He then bounced the balls further away, so I had to use my feet. Every moment of the lesson was meant to bring me success. Although I wasn't always able to catch the ball or hit it with my tennis racquet, we always finished every skill on "a good one".

After my first lesson, it was hard to wait for the second. I was hooked. I felt like I was making progress in some physical activity for the first time in my entire life. Although I may not have had a natural talent for sports, it didn't mean I couldn't learn some skills. This seems like a simple lesson but it took me nearly thirty years to learn.

Your fixed mindset may be something you have used well in the past. So why change it? It worked for you so why should it not work for your family and students? No matter how successful you are, think about what life could have looked like if you had a growth mindset.

Children learn from their role models. It is essential to have a growth mindset if you want to make a positive impact on their lives and ensure that they are mentally healthy.

Are you able to identify yourself as having both mindsets? Are you able to display different mindsets in different areas? It is possible. This is not an all-or nothing situation.

My family believed it was crucial to be right. If you weren't, you were wrong, and that was the same as losing. There were many arguments and struggles to prove that we were right, as you can see.

This attitude was carried into adulthood and I married someone who shared my beliefs.

My husband suggested once that I wasn't as smart as he because I was not as intelligent.

He was only a teacher, but he was also a lawyer. Later, he claimed that he wasn't being serious but I took it as a serious comment because of my mentality. My intelligence was being questioned. This was a huge blow to my confidence, as I was already anxious about not being as intelligent as my siblings.

My reaction was not pretty. Instead of telling him calmly that I disagree, I started to rant and rave. This was an extreme overreaction because I believed what he said to be true deep down. My fixed mindset shifted into high defensive mode.

This event is still a part of my life because it made me tired and inspired me to think about how I could prevent the same thing from happening again. Although I knew I was smart, my fixed outlook meant that I didn't believe this. To preserve my image, I decided that it was time for me and my husband to stop comparing. My brain retained the fixed mindset thoughts even though I stopped voicing them. To spark this change, I had to go on a walk with my kids.

My two young children asked me if I could take them for a walk and observe the horses in a field. I thought I'd take a minute to teach my daughter about the horses and she replied that there were five. She replied, "Five." She answered three so I asked her to count them all with me. After we reached three, she pointed out the opposite side of the field to me and asked, "What about the ones under the tree?" There were two more I didn't know about.

My children were right and I was wrong. As I struggled to find a solution, I had an Ah-ha moment. My children didn't judge me for making a mistake; they didn't care that I hadn't seen the horses under the tree. It was fine to be wrong. I resolved to look closer, not be so sure I was right the next time, and recognize that my mistakes didn't make me a less person. I wasn't less loved or more effective because I didn't see two horses.

The first step in any kind of transformation is awareness. Carol Dweck's book was not yet available to me, but I realized that certain ways of looking at life weren't serving me well. It was okay to be wrong. This didn't reflect my intelligence or who I was as an individual. The book Mindset had a profound impact on me because it outlined the beliefs that I had already developed when I became a mom.

You can't hear the advice and lessons that others offer, but you won't listen if you have a fixed mindset. Failure is an opportunity to learn. You believe success is about being better than your competitors, putting in effort, and failing to do so means that you are a failure.

The Principle

Your mindset is the way you see and perceive your world and how you think about it. A growth mindset is one that believes intelligence and potential are just starting points and that you can learn more and become smarter over time. This attitude will make you more resilient and happy if you don't fear failure, challenges, or risk.

This mindset is fixed and assumes that every person is born with the same intelligence and abilities. This belief makes you more concerned with your appearance than the journey and lessons you're learning. You don't want to improve your intelligence if you think you're not very intelligent. A fixed mindset makes it much more difficult to be strong and happy.

Action

1. These mindsets can be illustrated using movies and storiesThis is a great way to reinforce and teach the mindsets. You want to find strong

characters who can overcome all odds and succeed by learning. Seabiscuit and Groundhog Day provide good examples.

Caution: The Tortoise and the Hare is an age-old tale that children often hear and read. Although the moral of the story states that slow and steady wins, how many people can identify with the tortoise or wish to be treated as such? It is important to look for stories that children can identify with. If you are a rigid thinker, the tortoise may be seen as someone who was born with very little talent but has had a fortunate break that made him a winner.

You can add English lessons to help you understand the mindsets of characters in books that you're already reading. This is more about tweaking the activities and questions you already use than creating a new curriculum.

2. Choose a growth mindset

You can begin to recognize the difference between these two beliefs once you have a better understanding. Start by reframe your thoughts and stopping to understand the differences. As a school or family group, you can help each other identify when you have stuck to fixed beliefs.

You can practice recognizing different mindsets by watching the people you meet. You don't have to judge others about their lives or make bad choices. However, observing other mindsets can help you recognize when you are losing sight of your true purpose and allow you to take steps to change your thinking. Be an observer and not a judge.

3. Life is an adventure, with ups and downs.Take advantage of every opportunity to learn from all the things that happen on your journey.

4. All change can be made by making a choiceIf your partner doesn't want to change their mindset, you can't tell them. This shouldn't stop your partner from modeling the growth mindset or sharing information about its benefits in order to inspire others to live a happier lifestyle.

5. With a growth mindset, react to report cardsBe more concerned about your children's effort scores than their letter grades when they bring home their report cards. While you may not always get an A, you can still try your best. You will become more skilled and smarter the harder you work and the more you practice. Ask your child to explain why they are not achieving the best grades.

Encourage growth mindset through feedback. Instead of focusing on intelligence and natural abilities, comment on their accomplishments, effort and growth. Precept #3 will discuss praise.

Conclusion

How happy you feel will depend on how you see your life. A growth mindset can help you feel more positive. Instead of seeing failure as a defeat, see it as an opportunity for growth. People who are happy and able to learn from failures are more likely to be resilient.

Before you can change your mind about how you see life and learning, you need to be aware of what you are thinking. I know firsthand the benefits of having a growth mindset. Because I no longer feel the need to project the image I had to the world, I'm much more open-minded and tolerant. A new sense of calm has resulted from my learning to not judge others or their journeys. While I might not agree with their decisions, if they don't harm me, others, or their physical well-being, then who am I to judge them?

Carol Dweck's book, and my research on it, changed my life. It changed my perception of the world and gave me a better understanding of myself and the path I am on. You must have a mindset that is positive and will lead you to a happy, successful life.

Precept #3

Make Decisions & Take Responsibility

There are many choices in life: what to wear, how to eat, and what to spend your money on. Yet, many people still feel uncomfortable making decisions. This can be due to a lack practice, a fixed mindset and fear of responsibility for negative outcomes.

The Decision-Making Process

You may not be aware that decision-making is a continuous brain process. When it has to make a decision, your brain must go through complex analysis and evaluation. There are many opportunities for you to make decisions throughout your day. While some decisions are made with conscious thought, others are not.

Taking Responsibility

Responsibility is the other side of decision-making. You must be open to taking responsibility for the outcome of your choice. It's easier if you're happy with the outcome. But it's more difficult if it's not, especially if it affects others.

People who take rash decisions and don't consider the consequences may be more likely to make poor decisions. Knowing that you are responsible for your actions can help you make better decisions. It is a great mantra to remember: "The buck stops at here.".

If you don't want the responsibility of the outcome of your choices, then becoming a decision-avoidance specialist may be the best strategy.

My family was full if fixed-minded people. As being wrong meant you were less intelligent than someone who was right, this led to a lot more arguments. This made it risky to make decisions. I knew there was always a right way, so I wanted to be sure I chose the right one. My fear of making a wrong decision made it difficult for me to make decisions that would affect another person.

How Decision-making Increases Happiness

Both the Self-Determination Theory as well as the Needed Nine include autonomy. It's the ability to be independent and self-governing. You must believe that you have the power to make your own decisions and choices in order to feel content.

Accepting that you are responsible for your decisions is the key. This is easier if you're choosing one flavor of potato chips. It can be more challenging if you have been offered multiple jobs and are unsure which one you should accept.

It can be difficult or even impossible to make the right decisions when you're young. It is possible to avoid making decisions and give the responsibility to someone in your life. You may feel that you are no longer able to make the decisions. You may feel that your misguided loved one is doing you a favor by taking on the decision-making role in your life. It can be hard to take back control if this becomes a routine.

Your students and your children will be happier if they learn how to make decisions and deal with the consequences. Start young, making small decisions and increasing their importance as they grow older.

Micromanaging doesn't make one happy. But suddenly being forced to manage the world when you turn majority is not a good idea. Begin small and allow the skill to develop until the individual involved feels comfortable with the decision-making process as well as taking responsibility for the outcome.

Decisions and the Mindsets

Fixed

Growing up, I had a fixed mentality and was paralysed by fear of making any decision, especially if it affected another person. Because I believed that there were always win-lose situations in the world, pressure was constant to make sure I was on my side.

Because I left all the decision-making to my friends, they must have thought that I was a complete nightmare. This behavior was modeled by my mother. My mother was also uncomfortable with making decisions. I realized the value of sharing decision-making responsibilities with others only after I was older. Although I believed I was being easygoing, in reality I was trying to avoid taking responsibility for making a wrong choice.

You are giving up control over your life if you don't make the decisions. This reasoning works well if you have a fixed mindset. If you don't make any decisions, you don't have to take any responsibility.

While this may seem like a safe approach, it's not healthy. To live a mentally healthy lifestyle, you must make choices and take responsibility in a non-judgemental manner.

Fixed mindsets make it difficult for people to take responsibility for their mistakes. They feel that they are being labeled by the decisions they make. You are a winner if you make a winning choice. But a loss is an unacceptable outcome. This mindset will allow you to see the world as both winning and losing.

These people find that blaming someone or something else is the best way to deal with bad decisions. Your equipment was not good enough to make the shot. The teacher asked unfair questions that were not covered in class. You scored low on the exam. Fixed mindsets try to prevent them from being held responsible for failing to make a correct decision.

Growth

People with a growth mindset find that making decisions isn't as frightening and can be done without fear. It becomes a skill that improves with practice.

If you see failure as an opportunity for learning, you won't be afraid to make decisions and take responsibility. If you make a thoughtful decision, what's the worst thing that could happen? You might not be able to make it work. It might not work out. However, you'll still be able to learn about yourself and the world around.

People with a growth mindset are not afraid to fail and they are open to taking risks. Even if you are just making a pizza topping choice, every decision involves some risk.

You don't have to worry about being viewed negatively if you live and learn with a growth mindset. Your ego doesn't care if you are labeled a failure because of a bad decision. You made the wrong choice.

This view gives children a significant advantage over their more fixed-minded counterparts. They are able to explore the world and make choices, while being strong enough take control of their actions. They understand that their decision doesn't define who they are as individuals.

Validation

Validation refers to the need for approval or reassurance. Are you satisfied with the choice that you have made?

Who are you most likely to turn to for validation? Are you looking for external validation from family, friends and colleagues or are you looking to you? If you feel that you made the right decision regardless of what others think, you are relying upon internal validation.

If you want to live happier lives, this is the type of reassurance that you should seek.

You may need validation in order to feel confident that you have made the right decision. Although it sounds innocent enough, when you become dependent on others for validation, you stop taking control of your life. You may end up following the advice of others. If you want to live a life full of happiness, there are many problems.

Consider Precept #1 of The Modeling Happiness Process. You are the only person who can see your journey. You must take ownership for your journey if you want to feel happy. This means being responsible for your actions and the outcomes. You may not choose the right path if you require approval from others.

Ask others you trust and respect for their opinions when you are faced with a major decision. You should gather information and make the right decision. Trust that you made the best decision at that time, based on what you knew. Don't worry about whether others agree. You can take responsibility for your decision and learn from it, no matter what.

Validation and the Mindsets

If you are a fixed thinker, it is easy to look for validation from others. External validation is important to ensure that your decision is correct. External validation means that you don't have to be responsible for the outcome if you don't achieve the desired result. If someone tells you that a failed decision was a good choice, it is them who are responsible. This mindset makes it easy to avoid taking responsibility.

This behavior is common in our society. You can see this behavior in action by watching athletes interview after losing a match or game. You are likely to see someone who is fixed if they talk about poor refereeing calls, feeling sick, or other reasons for their loss. They must find a cause for their loss that does not involve them.

These athletes see themselves as in a win-lose situation. If the fact that they didn't succeed reflected on their abilities, then they would have the courage to admit to the world and themselves that they were a failure. This is not an option. They find other reasons to play below their best standards, reasons that don't reflect on them negatively.

The growth mindset of athletes hates losing as much as the other. However, they can take a look at the situation and learn from it. They are not afraid to admit that their opponent is better or that they have underperformed. Failure at the moment is not the same thing as failure.

Stephen 'tWitch" Boss, a superstar contestant, is a shining example of someone who has a growth mindset. Before he was selected to be a finalist on 'So You Think You Can Dance,' he auditioned three times. He didn't give up on himself or label him a failure. Instead, he saw the rejection as an opportunity to practice and he was able to continue his training.

Poor workers blame their tools

The old saying "A person with a fixed mind" was certainly referring to someone who has a fixed outlook.

Praise

External validation can be strengthened by the kind of praise you received as a child or as an adult. If you're praised for your abilities and told that you can succeed when you succeed, it is a signal that you have a fixed mindset.

There is a downside to being praised for your abilities. What happens if you don't have the natural ability to do something? Does this mean that you have no natural abilities? Failure is a sign that you lack any natural abilities. The fixed mindset views success as something that comes from predetermined natural abilities. If you don't think you're smart today, you're not smart enough to be smarter tomorrow.

Teachers and parents often praise the ability of their children because they believe it will increase self-worth and confidence. This type of reinforcement, even though it is positive in the best of intentions can cause children to be afraid of making decisions. They are more concerned with not failing than they are about learning. Rather than boosting your confidence, praise can make you feel less confident.

Carol Dweck first suggested to me the idea that praise could cause problems for those who receive it in an article. Her article, "Caution - Praise can be Dangerous" shocked the world.

Dweck advises that you praise someone's effort and how far they have come. The growth mindset can be addressed when you place more emphasis on learning than natural talent.

Students were asked to solve ten difficult problems using a nonverbal IQ exam. This was part of a large study that involved hundreds of teenagers. Students who achieved similar success were awarded their marks and told that they had received a high score. Randomly, the students were divided into two groups. Half the students were praised because they were smart and the other half were praised because of how hard they worked to get their marks. There was a noticeable difference between the two groups when they were given new, challenging tasks that would allow them to develop their other skills. The task was rejected by those who were praised for their abilities, while those who were praised for their effort accepted the challenge.

Praise for ability can reinforce a fixed mindset and make people fear taking risks if they fail. If you have to learn it, you don't want the risk of trying something new. Those with a fixed mindset don't believe that exerting effort is necessary to improve their intelligence or natural abilities.

Appreciating effort and improving your performance is a way to foster a growth mindset. If you want happiness, this is the best mindset. It values effort and doesn't put pressure on you to do it perfectly the first time. Your ability to do well does not reflect your character. Your accomplishments do not define you.

You will learn to trust yourself and not depend on others for validation by making decisions. You are the one who has to live with the decision. This skill is rare. Do you feel confident enough to validate yourself and not be judged by your family or friends? This external validation is what I consider the greatest obstacle to happiness.

Trusting Your Gut

You have probably all made decisions based solely on gut feelings. Although you may not be able to pinpoint why something feels right, you know instinctively that it is. Teachers often encourage students to follow their instincts when answering multiple-choice questions. This strategy is scientifically supported.

The brain absorbs far more information than it can possibly comprehend. It can only process about 400 bits of that information, despite absorbing approximately 40,000 bits per second. This means that a lot of the information your brain receives doesn't reach your consciousness.

You may learn more by listening to lectures than you realize. This is why it's important to follow your instinct in multiple-choice exams. Your brain might know more answers than you realize.

One caution: You cannot predict the winning numbers of the lottery. The luck factor is more important than skill or understanding when it comes to winning the lottery.

Being Lucky

Some people consider themselves naturally fortunate, while others believe the opposite. Google defines luck as "success and failure caused by chance rather than one's own actions.".

Professor of Psychology in England Richard Wiseman became fascinated by luck and studied the differences between those who believed they were lucky and those who believed they were unlucky.

He chose one man who believed he was lucky, and another woman who thought she was unlucky. Both were invited to meet at a coffee shop. Both were directed to go to a cafe to get a drink and wait for a member to arrive.

The subjects were offered two chances to be lucky for something at each meeting. The five-pound note was placed directly outside the coffee shop. Inside, the only place the subject could sit was at a table with a successful entrepreneur.

Lucky person took the money and entered the coffee shop to buy a drink. The conversation led to a business opportunity. Unlucky person took the money and sat down with the businessman. He didn't have a conversation so didn't learn about the business opportunity.

Richard Wiseman derived these conclusions from many other studies and concluded that luck is your choice. This chapter is dedicated to making decisions. It's because one of his four principles of luck inspired me to mention it. Lucky people:

1. You are skilled in recognizing and creating opportunities

2. Listen to your intuition and make lucky decisions

3. Positive expectations can help you create self-fulfilling prophecies

4. You can turn bad luck into success by adopting a resilient mindsetTrusting your intuition and listening to it is the same thing as trusting your gut instincts. Your brain has processed more information than you could possibly know. Let your brain guide you to make the right decisions.

Helping with Decisions & Self-validation

Children are more inclined to seek validation from others than they are from themselves. They are often praised if they do something that parents or teachers approve of. Children may rely on others' opinions throughout their lives if they aren't taught to make right decisions, regardless of what others think. If you want to live a happy life, this is not a good place.

It is possible to grow up wanting people to like you. You might make decisions based on how they feel rather than what you feel. Did you ever do something you didn't really want to do just to make your partner smile?

It's okay to do good deeds for others even if they don't help you. But your motivation must come from you and not their belief that you should.

Letting Your Children Make Decisions

With practice, every skill can be improved. You will be more successful at making your own decisions sooner than you think. It is not easy to stand back and let your child fail - especially if your fixed mindset parent worries that your child will be negatively affected if they don't succeed in everything they try.

It can be difficult for parents to let go of their children enough to allow them to make their own decisions. There are several reasons why this is so. Your children may have different personalities or characteristics than you. It can be difficult to accept that your children may follow a different path than you. You might make different decisions than they do.

You may believe that parenting means protecting your children from negative situations. If you don't have a growth mindset and are able to teach your children how to make choices and take responsibility for their actions, you won't be doing them any favors.

Dweck conducted a study of middle school students transitioning. Many find this a difficult time because the work is harder, relationships between teachers and students are less important, and there are hormonal and physical changes.

This research examined students over a period of two years. There were many opportunities for middle school students, but those who had a fixed mindset were reluctant to take them on in the event of failure. They didn't want other people to see them working hard to succeed. And they didn't want to admit that they were struggling or ask for help. This attitude was detrimental to learning and led to children from this group doing less well in middle school than they did in elementary school.

The growth mindset students, on the other hand, seemed to thrive in the new environment and were more likely to achieve higher grades. They were not afraid of failure and took advantage every opportunity that was presented to them. They would seek out help if they didn't get it, then continue to try until they understood. They did not enter middle school thinking they had to know it all.

The transition from high school to college or university is another difficult step in education. It's much harder to get top marks in postsecondary education. Yet, many students who are working towards their degrees are used to getting straight A's. Many fixed-minded scholars can find it difficult to go from being a large fish in a small lake to being a small fish among a large number of high-quality fish. Research shows that people with a growth mindset are more likely to make the transition.

The Principle

A happy, fulfilled life requires making decisions and being accountable for the results. Your choices do not define you. This concept can be helped by developing a growth mindset.

There are many opportunities in life to make decisions. However, it can be more difficult for some people than for others. You may think you're better at making decisions for your kids than you are for yourself, but if they don't learn how to make decisions and take responsibility for their actions, it is a disservice. It is easier to make decisions when you have a growth mindset.

When faced with a difficult decision, gather information from other people but make sure that you are making the right choice. Do not rely on others' opinions to support your decision. Be confident in your conviction that you made the right decision.

Accept responsibility for your actions. If things don't go as planned, accept the consequences and seek out a lesson or unexpected benefit. This information will help you when you make a decision.

Action

1. Practice making decisions

   If you want to take control of your life, you must be able to make decisions. Although it may seem scary or uncomfortable to make decisions early on, you will eventually become more comfortable with it.

   2. Model good decision making skillsThis is essential if you want others to learn how to assess information and make the right choices. Children learn a lot from adults who influence them. To help students and their children make better decisions, it is important to share your decisions with them, even those that fail.

   Tell others about the difficult decision you made and how it felt to be criticized. It's a comforting way to show others that mistakes aren't always scary and that the best things can sometimes come from the worst.

   If your four-year-old refuses to wear a coat, but you believe they should, discuss the possibility that they might get cold. If they are stubborn, you can take the coat off. If you want your child to be responsible for their choice, it is crucial that you do not slip the coat into your bag.

CAUTION: If the temperature drops below freezing or they complain about being cold 15 minutes into an excursion, you would not do it. You might have to make a change if you are unable to guarantee a safe return home. Another way to let them make a decision is to inform them that they cannot ski if they don't wear their jacket.

Is it easy? No. Teaching your children life skills is more difficult than simply following the easy path. Listening to your children complain about being cold is more wearable than just carrying it around until they choose to. However, the easy route is often not the best way for them to become a happy, well-adjusted adult.

3. Do not provide a safety netIt is difficult, but it is possible. I have seen it happen.

Your child will believe that you are there for them no matter what. This does not teach independence skills. Although it can be difficult to let go of your children and allow them to make mistakes and become more independent, it is essential that you do so.

4. As they grow up, your children and students will make more decisions.Give your children and students more autonomy as they grow up and are able to make their own decisions. There are many ways to do this. Be creative according to the needs of your family and classroom. Offer them different perspectives and ideas, but let them know that the final decision is up to you. They will have to live with the result. If you accept responsibility for the decision, you will also be responsible for any consequences.

My high school best friend and I worked together in summer camp at our parents' campsites. My friend received $2,000 in wages at the end of her season. She was given $2,000 as her wages for the season.

My family didn't give me any money. My parents were the ones who would give me money if I had a need. My clothes and personal expenses were paid for by my parents. However, I was able to receive an allowance to help with small purchases. My parents probably spent as much on me as my friend's parents on her. However, they were able to control what was bought.

Although I was pleased with the arrangement, it was still a difficult decision for me to make. I didn't want the responsibility of making mistakes. My friend was able to do it herself. She would be able to budget more effectively if she made a mistake or ran out of money. Her family did not rush to her rescue.

Which was the best approach to adulthood?

5. Sleep on it

I advise others and myself to rest when faced with a difficult decision. Rest seems to help me clarify my thoughts after I have considered all of the options, but still remain unsure which way to go. Sometimes, when I wake up, I get a gut feeling that tells my which decision is right. This is what I discovered when I began researching the book.

Many studies have looked at the effects of sleeping before making big decisions. Many studies suggest that if you only use your conscious mind to assess facts and make a decision, it may be more sure that you made the right decision.

Your subconscious mind can help you make important decisions when you are faced with difficult decisions. Researchers asked participants to select from a variety of cars in a study published by the Journal of Consumer Psychology. Participants were provided with information on safety ratings, gas mileage, and additional features such as cup holders or sunroofs.

Some subjects were allowed to rest on the information and some were asked to decide immediately. Researchers wanted to find out how many people choose a quality car rather than one that has a lot of bells and whistles, which can lead to poor gas mileage and poor safety ratings. 90% of participants who decided to sleep on it chose a quality car. Only 75% of those asked to make the same decision immediately.

Your subconscious mind can be described as a massive memory bank that has virtually unlimited storage. Your brain cannot process all of this information. Therefore, whatever information it doesn't have to pass on to your consciousness, it stores in your subconscious storage bank. It is here until it is required.

6. Praise those who do good

Instead of applauding intelligence and ability, praise learning and progress instead. Do not let admiration and praise push the recipient into a fixed mindset that makes it harder for them to live a robustly happy life. To increase the happiness of the receiver, praise should be used that encourages growth.

Conclusion

You need guidance when you're young. However, it is important to have the ability to make decisions and to live with them. This is how you can take control of your own life. Parents can feel terrible when their children fail. But remember, you are there for support, not control. Your children and students will be better off if you let them fail and help them to overcome it.

This is a difficult situation, and I can attest to it from personal experience. However, taking the first step at five is better than doing so at twenty-five, when the stakes may be higher and the ground is further away. My brother used to tell me this as he tried to ensure that my son got his high school assignments in time. It is better for him not to take a grade 10 class than to complete one that is essential for his university degree. It is true but it can be difficult to watch and wait. Sometimes, we have to allow others to fail before they can move on to the next stage of their journey. Sometimes, even though things seem to be falling apart it could be that the pieces are falling into place.

Instead of looking to others for validation, look to yourself. Only you can see the whole picture and understand the journey that you are on. Encourage your children and students to not only consider other opinions but also to trust their own ability to make decisions. Your life is yours alone, so make sure it's the best one.

This book will encourage you to choose happiness. Although you might be happy, if you don't choose to live that way, it could be that you are living with a fragile form of happiness. Is it possible for your fragile well-being to be ruined by a bump in life? This is what happened to my life when I moved from Canada to Britain. I didn't make the decision to be happy so I didn't know how to restore it.

Be confident in your ability to make decisions. Then, take responsibility for them. Understanding that you have the option of not making decisions if making decisions is hard for you is an option. You are responsible for your own life.

Precept 4 – Change Your Perspective

While you might think that your eyes see, your brain actually sees. Your optic nerve transmits information from your retina into your brain where it interprets the images.

Optical Illusions

One day in junior high, I was shown a picture with both a young and an older woman's faces. At first, I couldn't see the younger one. But with some help from my teacher, the second was clearly visible.

You may have seen it or something similar. Another famous one has a candlestick and two faces in profile. One image is easy to see, while the other one takes a bit more effort to find.

These optical illusion picture duos are clearly a mirror of life. Although you might initially interpret the events in this way, it is possible to see another way if you take enough time to consider. Is the glass full or empty? The glass is half full if it contains exactly half of its volume in water. No matter what viewpoint you take, the same information is sent to your mind. Your brain is ultimately responsible for the interpretation of the water content of the glass.

It is up to you to decide if it should be seen half-full or half-empty.

Optimist or Pessimist?

Are you able to learn from it?

Are you a cashier or customer service representative?

Is your glass half-full or half-empty?

Each of these three questions has more than one answer. If you want happiness, it is important to understand that you have choices in how you interpret your life.

National Taiwan University psychology researcher Sophie Chou discovered that realistic optimists are more successful than pessimists and people who are unrealistically optimistic. According to The Mail Online, a realistic optimist is someone who sees the positive side of life but also has a realistic view of the future and what life holds for them.

Many pessimists will tell you that they don't believe in negativity, but they just want to be realistic. The optimist is being realistic, even though this is true. Both perspectives can believe they represent a different view of life. Only 400 of the approximately 40,000 bits of information that your brain receives are processed. How does the brain know what information to store and what it should process?

Your brain is programmed to support your beliefs and thoughts. Your brain will only process information that supports your belief that it will work out. Your brain is constantly working to support your beliefs. This is why people may see things differently in different situations. Your perspective can be changed to make it more positive.

Janitor or Caring Professional?

Amy Wrzesniewski, a psychologist, decided to examine how people who work in mundane jobs deal with being seen as unwelcome.

Interviews were conducted with cleaning staff in large hospitals throughout Midwest America. The results were in line with the expectations of our research team. They were consistent across all but one hospital. The janitors in this facility didn't view themselves as part of the cleaning crew; they saw themselves more as professionals who care for others. They saw their work as more than just cleaning. They also supported families visiting them in many small but important ways. They provided Kleenex and water as needed and were always available to listen. One worker said that they changed the photos in the rooms of the comatose patients to help them recover.

They were still cleaning floors and bathrooms and performing all other tasks assigned to janitorial staff. But they had a new perspective on the work they did. Instead of seeing their job as an unimportant, mundane task, they believed that it was making a difference in people's lives.

Choosing a Lucky Perspective

Take a look at the study Richard Wiseman created for the lucky man or the unlucky woman. These two people had equal opportunities but only one took advantage. The woman believed she was unlucky, so she saw life through a lens that emphasized the things she considered unlucky. However, the man believed that he was fortunate and he did so because of his faith.

Wiseman's further research revealed that people who consider themselves lucky are always looking for opportunities in their environment. People who believe they are lucky are more likely to have conversations with strangers. You never know who you might meet, or what may happen.

The Principle

You are not in control of many things that can affect your life. While you cannot control what happens, you can choose to react. Either you look for the hidden benefits of challenges or you complain and blame others. Although hidden blessings may not always be obvious, when you reflect on difficult times, it is possible to see that you have learned a new skill, expanded your comfort zone or gained an inner strength.

If you are feeling unjustly treated by others, change your outlook. Instead of reacting negatively, give them the benefit the doubt. It is impossible to know the details of someone else's lives. They may be reacting in a way they cannot control and you are merely observing. Your life will be transformed if you adopt a more calm approach and give others the benefit of doubt.

It is up to you how you see the events happening around you. It takes practice to prevent a negative cloud from falling, but it is well worth it if you want to live a life of robust happiness.

Action

1. Be a role model

Share with others your perspectives on situations. Talk to others about the reasons they might choose to cut you off while driving. It can be easier to accept the actions of other drivers by trying to view it from their perspective.

2. Look at optical illusions

See how the same image may be seen in multiple ways.

3. Photos of signs such as pedestrian crossingWhat could the sign be indicating? Encourage creativity.

4. Make and/or view a kaleidoscopeDiscuss the possibilities of combining pieces in different ways to create different patterns. This is a new way to look at the same objects.

5. Create Tangrams

Puzzles can be used in many ways to create different shapes.

6. Try different perspectives on eventsYou can use real-life situations or characters from stories. You can brainstorm the unexpected benefits of facing challenges. Try looking at an unpleasant interaction from a different angle.

7. Look for the humor in difficult situationsThe best way to handle embarrassing situations was to remind yourself that they would make great stories for the next time you entertain your family or friends.

8. You can watch Pollyanna or read her and then play the Glad Game.Although the main character is sweet and sour, she is actually on the right path when it comes to seeing events through a different lens. She is trying to be happy.

9. Give others the benefitIf your first instinct is to judge others, you might try looking at the situation from a different perspective.

10. Learn from difficult experiencesWhat can you learn from a negative experience that isn't positive? What can you learn from a negative experience?

Conclusion

It is up to you how you see the world. You can't control the external circumstances but you can choose how you react. Use the Pollyanna Principle to find something positive from what happened or a lesson that you can learn from the difficulties you face.

Give people the benefit of doubt instead of thinking badly about them. Look for the good in whatever you experience, no matter what the difficulties or failures. This will help you create a life with more positives than negatives. It is possible to not immediately see the positives from negative experiences.

Sometimes it takes time and effort to learn from a seemingly bad experience. Do not rush. Trust that you will find something useful at some point.

You can help yourself and others to change the way they see themselves and their surroundings. Even if you have a negative inner voice, this attitude will help you to model. When my daughter was growing up, I didn't eat a 'diet. When I felt the need, I changed my diet to make it healthier. I did not want her to believe that it was normal for women to starve to lose weight. Although it was an enjoyable exercise, I struggled with my inner demons throughout the process.

People who are struck by circumstances many others would shudder under have made some of the most positive and cheerful people I've ever met. When I think about these situations, my mind immediately goes to a young boy with broken bones. He was an optimistic, caring, and positive child, despite his very serious illness. He didn't dwell on his circumstances, he accepted it and lived life to its fullest.

There are many ways to look at any situation. Even when it is difficult, there are lessons to be learned. A positive outlook will lead to a life full of happiness.

Precept 5 – Be Curious

Jean Piaget, a Swiss psychologist, defined curiosity as the desire to understand the unpredicted. It is the desire to know more about yourself and the world around. Your natural curiosity is what you were born with. It helps you grow and learn. Unfortunately, many people lose their natural curiosity as they get older, which can lead to a loss of motivation to learn and grow.

What is stopping our natural curiosity? Research shows that the decrease in curiosity is linked to our awareness of how others evaluate us. Many children go to school eager to learn new things and are curious sponges. Report cards don't rate the number of ways that you can make noises using your chair in a variety of ways highly. It is more important to reach the goals set by the teacher than to learn.

The Problem with Comparison

I have already written about how awful I was at team sports while I was in school. My only relief from the feeling of failure in this field was when another student joined the school, who was either as bad or worse than me. Although it didn't happen very often, it was something that made me feel happy. It was comforting to know that someone had worse skills than me. Although I may be a failure, there are others who have been more successful than me.

Comparing yourself to others is, for the most part a negative activity. Comparing yourself to others is a way of proving that you are doing well, or at least that you are doing better than another person.

Fixed mindsets are more concerned about comparing themselves to others in order to preserve their image. A growth mindset is less concerned with how others compare to you and more focused on your own learning journey.

Comparing others can lead to inaccurate perceptions of their true situation. It may seem that everything is perfect from your perspective, but this may not always be true.

You might think of the old saying, "The grass is always greener where I am standing." However, you won't be able to see the grass in your lawn, crab grass, weeds, and sparse patches. It may look different if you stand in someone else's grass.

Comparing yourself with someone who is doing better can lead to a lot of harm. Remember that you don't know the inner workings of someone's life until you live it.

Competition or Collaboration?

The mindset you adopt has a lot to do with how successful you are at collaboration. This is an important skill to possess when you are part of a team. Putting the success of the group, or family, ahead of your own individual achievements is necessary if you want to create a cohesive unit. Constantly comparing yourself to others and trying to make sure you are the winner is a disaster when it comes to working cooperatively.

The fixed mindset looks for comfort in finding someone with grass that is worse than their own, constantly checking to see how they stack up against the accomplishments of others. They see life as a series of competitions where only one person can win, so being part of a team can prove challenging and frustrating. What if the others don't want to use your ideas? How can you appear all-knowing if someone else's ideas are considered to be better than yours?

Unless everything you do within the group can be accomplished with the appearance of effortless brilliance, the person with the fixed mindset may well prefer to do nothing at all. When times get tough, the fixed mindset tends to give up. This can cause animosity in teamwork situations, rather than creating a group of cohesive individuals that are working together towards success.

With a growth mindset, you are better prepared to be part of a team. You tend to seek win-win scenarios, and are less concerned about comparing yourself to others. A win for the team is a win for you. This makes collaborative work easier to participate in successfully.

Curiosity and the Aging Brain

Not that many decades ago, it was believed that brains developed and grew until a certain age, and then the brain cells slowly started to die off. You expected that as you aged, you would become less able to learn new things, find your existing skills diminishing and your brain working less efficiently. New research has discovered that this is not the case at all.

Scientists are learning that the human brain has a much greater capacity for learning and development than anyone ever thought possible. The study of neuroplasticity shows that the pathways in our brains can develop and strengthen, even as we age. Your brain is like a muscle; the more you use it, the stronger it gets; the less you use it, the weaker it gets.

Constantly improving your skills, regardless of how advanced they already are, is the behavior of a life-long learner. Why do professional athletes continue to get coaching, even though they may already be ranked number one in the world? They are striving to continue improving, even if it is by the smallest of margins. Setting goals and working to achieve them is one of the needed nine elements of happiness, as well as an intentional activity referred to in the Happiness Equation.

Curiosity and School

I did well in my post-secondary courses. I learned how to listen to the professor and parrot back their values and viewpoints. This resulted in good grades, but not necessarily in becoming more knowledgeable or more skilful. The school system would be so much better if we could encourage more love of learning, and less reward for getting the right answer.

Every year curious children start school, only to discover the world of letter grades. When they are rewarded with an A, parents and teachers smile, say well done and shine the spotlight on them. This is especially true if you are working with fixed mindset teachers or parents.

Suddenly your curiosity for learning has competition. Many children stop learning because they are curious, and instead start focusing on getting a good letter grade. Their motivation changes completely; they want validation from the adults in their lives. They would rather complete activities they know they can do and which will result in a good grade, instead of nourishing their curiosity and choosing a more challenging path that will help them learn more.

The curious mind has a much better chance of surviving the school years intact if its owner has a growth mindset, as these minds value learning over the need to get good grades and receive external validation.

Individual Learning Rates

At birth, your brain is only partially developed. Knowing as we do that brains change every time they learn something or practice a skill, it shouldn't surprise you to discover that brains develop at their own pace. If you look at ten twelve-year-olds, you will see a huge range in height, weight, and physical development. We accept that without much thought, but would it surprise you to discover that there is just as much variation in the development of their brains?

Everything you learn and do creates physical changes in your brain. The pathways that are created or reinforced are different for each of us. We all experience life differently and thus the way our brain wires itself is unique. This is also true for identical twins, even if they are sharing the same experiences.

As parents and teachers, you need to bear this in mind when you are interacting with children. To expect that everyone of the same age will be ready to learn the same skills is like suggesting that everyone should reach puberty by the time they are twelve. It is unrealistic.

This is another reason the growth mindset makes learning more rewarding. Being slower to develop some skills doesn't label you as slow, nor does it suggest that you won't ever be as talented as your compatriots, who may have mastered the same skills at a younger age. Students need learning environments that respect individual differences and give more credit to effort than being an early learner. A child who is one of the youngest in his year, or grade, at school, can be at a huge disadvantage in the fixed mindset world.

How Curiosity Increases Happiness

Having an opportunity to use your abilities is one of the features that creates feelings of positivity about school and work.

This feature addresses two sides of your abilities: the skills you already possess, and the opportunity to gain new ones. It is part of human nature to enjoy doing things that you are good at. Most people find it enjoyable to participate in activities where they already feel comfortable and somewhat competent.

I was never very good at sports, but instead of practicing shooting a basketball I would spend my time reading or creating music. Those were things I was good at and enjoyed, so they were the abilities I invested myself in. Perhaps I should have been improving my basketball skills, but that doesn't fit with human nature. The kids who spend all their time shooting hoops are more likely to be the ones who are already reasonably good at it, or at least *see* themselves as being good at it. Remember, perception is key.

Because we feel happier when we are doing things we believe we are proficient at, being given the opportunity to use these abilities will give you a huge boost of satisfaction.

Attaining new skills is also important if you want to increase your happiness. Research consistently shows that people who continue to learn new skills have a greater level of satisfaction. It is also increases confidence and self-validation.

The actual process of learning a new skill may not be a painless one, however. Ryan Howell, an assistant professor at San Francisco State University, calls it the 'No Pain No Gain' rule. Although the initial process of learning something new may cause you to feel stressed while you are doing it, you will feel happy and satisfied when you look back after having become successful at it. Keep this in mind the next time you want to quit before you master a new competency. You need to suffer through the pain to gain the happiness.

Remember that your brain is creating and strengthening neural pathways whenever you work on new skills. Rather than giving up, picture what is happening in your head and rest assured that the struggle will be worth the effort.

The Principle

Happy people are life-long learners. Constantly finding opportunities to learn new things comes from a sense of curiosity. You were born with a very inquisitive nature, but unless you were encouraged to nurture it, it may well have disappeared, at least to some degree.

Rediscover your spirit of curiosity by honoring effort and improvement, rather than effortless natural ability. Model a mind that is interested in new experiences, knowledge, and understanding. See wonder in the world around you, and strive to learn more about yourself and your environment. Modelling an inquisitive nature will encourage you to look for learning opportunities throughout your entire life.

Action

1. Be a role model

   Encourage your curiosity and make a commitment to learn new skills. If youngsters see adults continuing to ask questions about the world they live in, in order to learn more, they will be more likely to adopt these same attitudes as they grow into adulthood. Model your choice to be a life-long learner.

2. Brain Work

   Teach students about the brain and what happens to it when they learn.

   Use rope, string, thread, and other materials to demonstrate how neural pathways are created and strengthened as you learn new skills.

3. Honor Effort

   Praise effort rather than ability. Help students imagine what is happening in their brains when they are exerting effort or learning new skills.

Journal each day and ask students to record what they learned and what they had to work hard at.

Ask your children what they learned at school that day and what took effort for them to achieve. This is a great supper time activity, or a conversation to have on the way home from school if you are picking them up. Don't accept that they didn't learn anything, and if they said they didn't have to try to achieve anything, help them understand that they weren't strengthening their brains if they didn't have to work hard. Praise them for effort exerted rather than ability possessed.

4. Move Out of Your Comfort Zone

Provide opportunities and support that allow students to take a small step out of their comfort zone.

- Try a new game or sport
- Taste different types of food
- Share times when you stepped out of your comfort zone and lived to tell the tale
- Ask students who enjoy leaving their comfort zones to share their experiences and strategies
- Look for story characters who are out of their comfort zone. Discuss/write about what this person felt during and after the experience
- If appropriate, try a trust walk or trust fall activity
- Celebrate students who have tried something new or nerve-wracking

Conclusion

There is no reason for your curiosity to die as you grow older, but it does. We stop learning or striving for new goals, choosing instead to rest on our laurels and enjoy what we have already achieved.

To model happiness, it is vital that you rediscover your inquisitive nature. This will become easier if you ensure you are viewing the world with a growth mindset. Try something new without the fear of failure, set goals that are just out of your reach and then create a strategy to attain them, or take a few steps out of your comfort zone. As professional speaker Linda Edgecombe loves to say, 'When was the last time you did something for the first time?'

Precept 6 – Connect with Others

At the end of a long summer away from school, I asked my son if he was looking forward to getting back to class. He thought for a few moments before telling me he was excited to see all his classmates, but he really didn't want to go back to school.

This is not an unusual sentiment, and isn't limited to students. Have you ever had a job that you didn't really like, but you stayed with because you liked your colleagues, and felt like you were part of the team?

Dr. Brene Brown, a research professor at the University of Houston Graduate College of Social Work writes, 'A deep sense of love and belonging is an irresistible need of all people. We are biologically, cognitively, physically, and spiritually wired to love, to be loved, and to belong. When those needs are not met, we don't function as we were meant to. We break.
We fall apart. We numb. We ache. We hurt others. We get sick.'

It is important to recognize that feeling connected has nothing to do with the number of connections you have. More is not necessarily better. The key is to *perceive* that you have a link with another person. As with so many other topics you have read in this book, the key to success is *believing* you are connected, not in persuading others to think you are. If you feel attached to another person, it doesn't matter whether they view your friendship the same way or not. You will benefit from being connected.

Social Connection and Personality Types

There is variation in the amount and type of social contact different personality types need, but it is essential for everyone to have some level of social connection if they want to live a life of robust happiness.

There is a mistaken belief that introverts prefer to be on their own. This may be true to some extent, but even people who love their own company are hardwired to seek out the companionship of others. They may prefer to be around only a few people at a time, or avoid situations where they are expected to make small talk for extended periods, but everyone needs connections with others.

I love my own company and believed I was an introvert until I became Myers Briggs certified when I was in my early 50s. It turns out I am an extravert who changed schools a lot. With my fixed mindset that *knew* I wasn't very smart, I lacked the self-confidence necessary to put myself out there and risk rejection. How did I manage to feel connected when I moved schools so often and was timid when it came to making social links?

As a child, I was very connected with my family and I always made a few close friends each time I moved. As I entered adulthood, I still made sure I had family and close friends in my life, but I also got in the habit of striking up conversations with cashiers, other people waiting in lines, and random people whose paths crossed mine. I perceived a connection with each of these interactions. It didn't matter how the other person felt; I received a little jolt of positivity each time I created a short-lived connection. My perception of the interaction ensured that I felt connected.

The amount and type of social contact you desire is very individual. Some of you crave constant company, while others prefer to spend more time alone or interacting one-on-one. Some of you do your best work while being surrounded by the energy of other people. For others, hearing constant conversations means you are unable to get your work done. Regardless of where you fit in the scheme of social contact, you all need some interaction to be happy.

If you don't spend enough time with others, you may become lonely. If you spend too much time with them, you may become frustrated. Neither of these states is desirable. It is also important to consider the type of contact you are having. Negative interactions aren't going to foster a feeling of wellbeing. For some people, their greatest source of unhappiness is the people they network with.

Connecting in the World of Technology

No discussion on social connection and youth would be complete without addressing the role and impact of technology. There is no doubt that the way we interact has changed, but if we are going to be true to our species, we need to change along with our environment. I don't believe that cell phones and computers are going to disappear, so you need to find ways to work with them to nurture social connection.

Nothing can take the place of face-to-face interaction, but technology can be an aid to strengthening it. Have you ever watched a group of work mates bond in the lunch room by discussing a popular book, movie, or mini series? I've made amazing connections with other ladies who are Costco groupies. Shared experiences are incredibly powerful glue; you don't have to watch the program together to bond by discussing it. Playing online games with other people, especially if you have a face-to-face relationship with them as well, is still a type of social interaction. You are sharing an experience and communicating, even if you can't see them.

I feel much more connected with family and friends that don't live near me, because I keep in contact through Facebook. I have also made friends with people online before meeting them in person. When I met them for the first time, I already felt like I knew them. The online experience had created a connection that was then strengthened face-to-face.

Technology isn't necessarily a bad thing. It can help nurture relationships. The problem comes if you allow it to replace traditional relationships. As a role model, you can develop and demonstrate ways to use technology as a supplemental way to foster and strengthen friendships or business associations.

Researchers from the University of Florida surveyed 339 students to discover if using smart phones reduced their social capital. This expression is defined by Dictionary.com as 'the network of social connections that exist between people, which enable and encourage mutually advantageous social cooperation.' Even though participants reportedly spent 100-200 minutes a day on the internet and 30-90 minutes daily on social media, every one of them had a positive amount of social capital and weren't at all socially isolated.

At the other end of the age spectrum, studies looked at whether social media sites help seniors stay connected. Findings show that the participants benefited from better health, less chance of reduced cognitive skills, and longer lives if they used sites like Facebook. Only a small percentage of American adults over the age of 65 use Facebook. This may be in part because of the age they were at when social media became popular. Perhaps we should be encouraging seniors to start using social media now. It is never too late to learn a new skill.

The Happy Chicken & Socially Connected Egg

In the section on the Importance of Emotions, I shared with you how people who feel mildly to moderately happy find it is easier to make new friends. When you have friends, it is easier to feel happy, and if you are happy, you are more likely to make new friends.

Do you need social connections to feel happy, or do you need to feel happy first so you can make social connections? These elements are so closely linked that it is difficult to separate them, making it a chicken-and-egg type situation. Although you could debate which one came first, I don't think it really matters. The important thing is to understand that social connection is vital if you want to be happy.

> *One company I worked for provided Friday lunches if we made sales targets for the previous month. It was a great incentive, enjoyed by everyone. We didn't get much of a chance to gather together as a group during the work day, so these lunches helped us bond.*
>
> *One year, we missed the targets for February and because the shortfall was added to what needed to be achieved for the next month's target, there were no more Friday lunches – for the rest of the year.*
>
> *The change in moral and team spirit was overwhelming. Taking away the opportunity to strengthen our social connection did untold damage to the strength of the company.*

The Principle

Humans are social creatures with a basic need to spend time with others and to be accepted by them. It renews your sense of belonging and purpose. Connection is more than just being in the same space, it is about creating a link or relationship with another person. The more connected you feel, the happier you are. Having friends is a powerful force when it comes to happiness. You may be nervous about doing something by yourselves, but put a few friends by your side and chances are you will become a superhero.

Research shows there are many health benefits associated with being socially connected, including an increased immune system, lower levels of anxiety and depression, longer life-spans, and greater self-esteem. A landmark study by House, Landis and Umberson suggests that a lack of social connection negatively affects your health more than obesity, smoking and high blood pressure combined.

Action

1. Respect and honor your connections

   Model behavior that respects others and honors individual differences. This includes creating a non-judgemental attitude towards other people. Just because they do things differently to you doesn't mean their way isn't just as good as yours. If they aren't harming you or anyone else, there is no valid reason for you to stand in judgement.

2. Try to be a source of positive energy for the people you interact with

   Emotions are contagious. If you enter a room of happy people, you are likely to find yourself feeling happy. The same goes if you surround yourself with negativity. If you make a concentrated effort to be a source of positive energy, the people who meet you will benefit from it.

3. Create safe environments and accepting cultures

A safe environment where everyone is accepted will do wonders to put your students and children in the right mindset to learn. The negative emotions that arise from a hostile environment make learning almost impossible.

Make sure your home and school environments honor individual differences and accept that each person is on their own journey of learning. You don't need to be friends with everyone you work or go to school with, but you do need to feel accepted and safe.

4. Create connections with the people in your life

Spend energy getting to know the people you interact with. Find out a little bit about them, and let them get to know you, too. If you are a teacher, make a connection with every student you teach.

This can be a challenge if you are a subject teacher rather than a classroom teacher, but with effort, it is doable. I'm not suggesting that you need to be their best friend, but talk to them enough that you know what they like, what their hobbies are, and maybe a little about their home-life. Let them get to know a little bit about you too.

5. Ensure your students have opportunities to work with others in partner or group activities

Having an opportunity to get to know someone better can help create a positive - or at least more tolerant - connection between members of different social or personality groups. When group or partner work gets tough, remind students that they are building new and helpful neural pathways and learning skills that will serve them well when they get into the working world.

6. Choose to view others through a positive lens

Accept everyone even if they aren't people you would be best friends with. Look for ways to appreciate what they have to offer. When difficulties arise, look for win-win solutions, and remember to give them the benefit of the doubt.

7. Make family-time a tradition

Build family activity habits into your life. If everyone is accustomed to these events happening on a regular basis, you are less likely to stop connecting as a unit.

Conclusion

The importance of social connection in the classroom, staffroom and family unit cannot be underestimated. How happy you feel has a lot to do with your connections with others. Social connection was essential in order for humans in more primitive times to survive. Today, we are still wired to seek out relationships with others.

With suicide rates among youths accounting for almost one in four deaths, more attention needs to be devoted to the importance of ensuring that children have opportunities to connect with other people, as this is an excellent way to create happy people, living happy lives.

Connecting at School

As a teacher of children between the ages of eight and fourteen, I rarely had any difficulties with discipline. This was largely because I made a connection with every child I taught. I talked to them when issues arose and helped them to choose to stay within the accepted boundaries of behavior in my classroom.

It wasn't until I substituted in a school I had never taught in before that I realized just how important that strategy was for me to be a happy teacher. I was in a grade eight class in a private school, and for the first time in my history as a teacher, I struggled to keep behavior within acceptable limits. I decided that substituting was not the job for me, although had I continued to go into the school and concentrated on making connections with the students, I am sure I would have overcome the problem.

Connecting at Home

How you connect with your family is a very individual decision. I am not suggesting that my family is another version of the Waltons, but we still love spending time together. Let me give you some ideas of ways you can connect with your loved ones, by sharing a few of the ways we stayed connected, even during the teenage years.

We created family traditions when our children were young. On the weekends, we would find time to play board games together, go to playgrounds, and watch movies. Even though my husband frequently slept through the Disney favourites, we were all together in the same room, doing something as a family. My children are now in their early 20s and we still play board games and watch movies together. For some families, it is skiing or playing sports as a group. It doesn't matter what activity you choose as long as everyone is interacting and enjoying themselves. When it comes to board games, you may not feel like everyone is enjoying themselves when arguing, or tempers kick in, but helping your children learn to lose is a valuable skill. This is the perfect opportunity to reinforce a growth mindset.

We made the decision for our family not to have televisions in the bedrooms. I think of TV as a social activity, not as something to do by yourself. We watch, discuss, and sometimes argue while having a shared experience. When televisions are in bedrooms, the experience becomes very isolated and anti-social. Having televisions in shared areas means that you may watch programs you aren't really interested in, but knowing what your family is viewing and being able to join in conversations about favorite programs more than pays for it in my opinion.

The family rule is no cell phones or tablets at the table. If you get a message or call, you can wait until dinner is over to reply. I also use this rule when we are in the car together. When my daughter and I go shopping, I expect her to give her attention to me, not to her phone. If she has to respond to a message, she apologizes and keeps the time she uses for it to an absolute minimum. During family interaction times, the face-to-face relationships take priority.

Precept 7 - Take Action

Change only happens when you act. The importance of appreciating the distinction between having knowledge and putting strategies into action cannot be underestimated. Far too many people have a dream that never becomes reality because they are afraid to fail, or don't feel able to put their plan into action. The dream fades and becomes no more than a fantasy.

Taking even a small step towards a goal gives you the opportunity to make a dream come true. Many long journeys are made up of small steps. You don't have to travel the entire way in one fell swoop.

Choosing to act on the values and beliefs you hold is a vital part of transformation. The forces that you encounter in life are going to make a bigger impact on you if you are already in motion. Sitting at home by yourself, reading books about happiness, will not make you happier. You have to take the information you've learned, then go into the world and make it happen through your actions.

Tips to Help You Take Action

Plan

If you know the direction you want to travel in, it is much easier to take a path that will get you there. If you have no idea where you're headed, you are much more likely to wander aimlessly, or even just stand still. Decide what you want to achieve and come up with one or two things that will help you to bring it about.

'Just do it' is the tagline for Nike, but I think it should be a mantra for everyone. Getting started is just that: a beginning. You can modify your goal as you progress, if you decide it isn't quite right. Nothing is set in stone, and being adaptable is a skill that needs constant practice. Plan a route, and take your first step. You can adjust your course as you travel.

The One Percent Philosophy

Do you believe in the 'all or nothing' approach to life? I call this the 100% philosophy. It means that you either do things with total commitment, or not at all. Expecting to transform yourself into a happiness model within a short period may not be realistic, nor is it likely to occur without some bumps and dips in your journey.

With the 100% philosophy, you are likely to start your transformation with passion and determination. You may have initial success, but what happens when you hit it a bump in the road? You wake up one day to discover you just don't feel like being optimistic. You want to wallow in negativity and complain about your life.

This is when the 100% approach may let you down. Instead of your bad mood and lack of energy upsetting your efforts for one day, people with this philosophy often feel that by straying off the path, even just a tiny bit, it is no longer worth taking that route at all. One slip and all positivity and growth mindset strategies are quickly and completely forgotten. You return to your previous attitudes and behaviors.

These people have created such a high standard for themselves that any weakness or detour means they have failed in their attempt to achieve that goal. Rather than seeing failure as an indication of something they need to continue to work on, they give up. If they can't do something unerringly, then they might as well not do it at all. Do you recognize the fixed mindset in this behavior?

I am not the type of person who sets the bar too high for myself, and for perhaps the first time in my life, I have found a reason why my 'good enough' approach might be better than the one held by my high-achieving, perfection-loving friends.

I'm not lazy, and I love to set and attain goals just as much as the next person, but I don't feel driven to be perfect. I am quite content to do what I can, and willingly accept that I will stumble from time to time. I don't lose a moment of sleep over it. Tomorrow is a new day and I am perfectly satisfied with taking small steps towards success.

I call this the 1% philosophy: from small changes come big differences. If you move forward, it doesn't matter how quickly or slowly you are going, just don't give up. In words from the Chinese classic text of Toa Te Ching,

The journey of a thousand miles begins with a single step.

The thought of dropping from a philosophy of 100% to 1% may horrify you, however I urge all of you one hundred percenters to join me. I like to think of the 1% approach as tweaking your life rather than changing it completely.

Do one little thing every day that will move you in the direction you want to go. Choose to give your friends the benefit of the doubt, add one intentional activity to your life, or decide to connect with one new person. Don't think every choice must be 100%; 1% is a viable, and sometimes preferable, option. Remember that one misstep only takes you a small way off your path; you can easily find your way back to the original trail.

The Serenity Prayer Philosophy

God grant me the serenity to accept the things I cannot change;
Courage to change the things I can
And wisdom to know the difference

I know I included this prayer earlier in the book, but its sentiment is important to remember when you are considering action. Worrying, fussing, and feeling frustrated about things you can't change is a waste of your time and energy. It is important to identify the things in your life that you have both the desire to change, and that *can* be changed. This takes conscious thought and reflection. The more you practice recognizing the difference between the things that can be altered and those that can't, the easier it becomes.

Some people like to bemoan what is happening in the world, but aren't prepared to do anything about it. I have chosen not to spend my mental energy worrying about things I'm not prepared to try and change. I'm concerned with how we treat the earth, so I recycle, pick up litter and try not to waste energy by leaving lights on. I choose to take small steps that will make a difference if we all do them.

On the other hand, I have no control over who will be the next president of the United States, so I choose not to waste my time discussing it endlessly. Unless I'm willing to stand up and act, I try not to spend my energy focusing on events and people that result in pessimistic thoughts.

The things you are willing to take action on will not be the same as everyone else around you. Choosing which battles are worth fighting is a very individual decision.

Be Wary of Unrealistic Expectations

How often do you find yourself disappointed in a movie that everyone else loved, or go to a party full of anticipation, only to find it wasn't as much fun as you had imagined? Modifying your expectations can increase your happiness.

I don't want anyone to think they can't aim high when they are setting goals; you should do exactly that, especially when it comes to your performance and accomplishments, but keep your expectations about how and when everything will fall into place realistic.

When I was on a commonwealth teaching exchange in my twenties, I decided I couldn't return home without a visit to Egypt. I didn't know anyone else who wanted to go, so I booked myself on to a tour. I didn't think being on my own would be a problem, because I assumed the tour would consist of a large bus full of English-speaking travellers. When I arrived in Cairo, I discovered that I was the only person on my tour. For some people that wouldn't have been a problem, but I was nervous about being in such a different culture all on my own. My expectations hadn't matched the reality I was given, and my first reaction was panic.

In actual fact, the time I spent in Egypt was a fabulous learning experience, and I discovered inner strength I never knew I had. Being disappointed isn't always a bad thing, but remember we are talking about happiness, and I'm pretty sure the happiest I was during that ten day Egyptian holiday was when I boarded the plane to return to England.

It is better to expect that the path you have chosen will have bumps and dips in it, rather than convincing yourself it will be paved and easy to walk along. Being pleasantly surprised by how well maintained the route is will encourage you to continue, while being disappointed in how much worse it is than you had imagined may leave you disheartened.

The Endowed Progress Effect

The first steps toward any goal are often the most difficult. I believe that the first step is always the hardest, especially if it involves stepping out of your comfort zone.

This Endowed Progress Effect was researched by Nunes and Dreze and suggests that when people feel they have made progress towards a goal, they are more likely to become committed to reaching it.

Have you ever found yourself staying at work later than you had planned, just so you could finish a report? You would be less likely to put that extra time into the endeavour if you were just starting out with the project. The closer you are to reaching a goal, the harder you work to achieve it.

If you are like me, you may think it is best to get the worst stuff out of the way first, but if you make the initial steps of your goal as easy to achieve as possible, you can put the Endowed Progress Effect to work. Save the more difficult steps until the end, when you are invested in the project. This can help you with the push you need to get the harder things done, rather than just giving up on them.

When you find yourself struggling to see a project through to the end, stop and reflect on how far you have already come. That mental reminder might be just the incentive you need to stick it out.

Live in the Moment

When you are working toward a goal, it is easy to focus on it so hard that you forget about what's already happening in your life. The same can be said about your past. You may have suffered through ordeals that affected you so much that you have trouble moving on from them.

Being consciously mindful of what is happening in your life *now* has been shown to help people:

1. Deal with long term medical conditions

2. Have lower levels of the stress hormone cortisol

3. Achieve greater emotional stability
4. Experience a better quality of sleep

Your body lives in the present, but your mind very rarely does unless you make a conscious effort to put it there. Happiness needs to be experienced, so it goes hand in hand with living in the moment. Don't let yourself become one of those people who plan on being happy at some point in the future, such as when they retire or find a new job. Make sure you are happy in the here and now.

My husband and I recently decided to go to Costa Rica. We love to travel, so the decision itself wasn't unusual. What made the choice a little bizarre was our decision to go even though we could only be there for four nights. We live on the west side of Canada where there are no direct flights to San Jose. Our adventure involved 3 flights each way, and an overnight on a plane or in an airport.

I started out being a little embarrassed to tell people our plans because it was so unconventional. The more I thought about it, the more I realized it was an adventure of a life-time, the sort of thing you tend to do when you are much younger. This was an impulsive decision. We could have put it off until we had more time to enjoy the country, but we didn't, we decided to have an adventure now.

Only being in Costa Rica for four days had some unplanned benefits. We were aware of how short our visit was, so we lived it to the fullest and enjoyed every minute of it. I had planned to work on this book while I was there, but that didn't go according to plan. My decision to enjoy our mini break is one I don't regret in the slightest, even though it put my book project behind schedule.

Having goals is important, but remember to balance your focus on the future with living in the now.

The Principle

Theory without action is just an interesting read. If you want to make changes in your life, you must act on the theories you learn. A precept is a principle that leads to action. I'm so happy you're reading this book, but if you don't ignite yourself into action, this movement to improve the mental health of young people won't get off the ground. Find ways to act on the precepts, building them into your life so you can model happiness.

Action

1. Start today

   Regardless of how nervous you feel about acting on your knowledge, there is no time like the present. You won't feel any less nervous tomorrow, so get started. Remember, the first step is often the most difficult.

2. Just do it

   Your plan doesn't need to be perfect before you act on it. For many people, waiting for the perfect plan toward a perfect goal is just a way of procrastinating, putting off the moment of getting started.

3. Increase Your Intentional Activity

   Add more happiness-boosting intentional activities to your life. The happiness equation shows this is the best way to feel a greater sense of well-being. Examples of ways to do this are:

   a. Commit random acts of kindness

      Have you ever seen someone struggling to open a door, or reach an item off the top shelf, and instinctively offered to help? How did aiding them make you feel? For most of us it is impossible to impulsively do something that benefits someone else without smiling and feeling a pleasant inner glow that lasts for longer than you might expect.

The benefits of performing random acts of kindness have been studied and research shows that doing an unexpected good deed makes us feel more positive. These deeds need to be initiated by the person who is carrying them out; they should not be something another person has told you to do. Having ownership of the act is important if you want to boost your happiness. Examples of random acts of kindness are:

i. Buy a coffee or muffin for the next person in line at the coffee shop

ii. Let someone merge into your lane even if the traffic isn't heavy

iii. Give someone a genuine compliment

iv. Over-tip your server

v. Let someone go ahead of you when you are waiting at the checkout

vi. Hold the door open for someone vii. Donate to a charity viii. Thank the bus driver ix. Smile at a stranger

b. Set, share, and celebrate your goals

Setting goals is important for many reasons that I have already talked about, but as well as setting them, you will increase your happiness if you share them, and celebrate accomplishing them.

Don't worry if you don't reach your goal. The boost of happiness comes from trying to attain them, so as long as you make every effort to do that, you will boost your good feelings.

If someone else knows your plan, you will be more invested in it. It is more difficult to give up when other people know what you are hoping to achieve.

Sharing your goals can provide you with support if you share them with the right people. Choose to tell friends, family, or colleagues who will listen and be there for you. I suggest you seek out people with growth mindsets.

Celebrations can be small. Take time to acknowledge your accomplishment, and let your support network join. Doing this will also increase your connection with your supporters.

c. Keep a journal

Reflection is an important part of the learning experience for adults, and a journal can help you do that. By recording your journey, you can see the progress you've made when times get tough and it feels like you haven't accomplished anything at all.

This is also the perfect place to record a daily intention and gratitudes. Both are intentional activities that boost happiness.

Record what you intend your day to be like. Remember that your brain only processes a small amount of the information it receives. Draw its attention to the things you want to see evidence of. Think about your intention throughout your day, and reflect on it at the end.

Think about, and if possible record, three things that you are grateful for every day. Choose different things as much as possible, and be specific about why you are grateful for them.

Encourage children to keep a journal. Journaling can involve drawing pictures, or writing in sentences, phrases, or keywords. It is never too early to start setting intentions and being grateful. This activity will also support learning to live in the moment.

4. Surround yourself with positivity

   Remember that moods are contagious. Make sure you are catching the positive ones, and providing happy moods for others to catch.

5. Take care of yourself

   What's good for the body is good for the brain.

   a. Exercise, eat well, and get plenty of sleep
   b. Take twenty minutes every day to do something for you
   c. Spend time outside regardless of the weather; taking a walk can make all the difference to how you feel

6. Adjust and adapt

   Stay mindful about your journey. Adjust your course and remain adaptable. Don't think that changing your direction is a sign of failure. You will be learning as you travel; using that new knowledge to make adjustments is the sign of a good navigator.

Conclusion

It may seem a little odd that one of the precepts is about action, when every precept is a principle that leads you to action, but actually getting yourself started is one of the most difficult things to do. All the knowledge in the world won't make any difference to your life if you aren't willing to act on it.

My own personal brand of procrastination involves the belief that knowing more will make the action I take even better. If I hadn't learned to recognize that pattern of behavior, I would still be at my computer now gathering data. I am still reading and learning, but I am also acting on my vision, not just thinking about it.

If you want to create change, you must act. The first step is the hardest, and while the subsequent steps aren't easy, they are easier. It's simpler to stay in motion than it is to put yourself into motion.

Thinking out of your comfort zone is a much less threatening activity, because no one has to know you are doing it. Stepping out of your comfort zone is an act that may be seen by others. Choosing to act on the information you gather is essential if you want to join the world of change makers. You must decide to be visible if you are going to be heard.

Precept 8 – Be Part of Something Bigger

We make a living by what we get;
We make a life by what we give.

Winston Churchill

I have a memory of watching the Oprah Winfrey Show many years ago, back when I was in my twenties. She said that the thing that made her happiest was her work with charities. This stuck in my mind, because it was something I had never considered before. As my life progressed, I heard this same sentiment from many other people. It wasn't until I was doing research for my first book that I found studies to support her statement.

Research supports giving as a powerful way to increase happiness and attain personal growth. A study on charitable giving showed that your brain reacts to altruistic acts in the same way it does to pleasure rewards. Both give you a warm glow that is associated with happiness. Studies also provide data that suggests we are hardwired to have a selfless concern for the well-being of others.

If you want happiness for an hour, take a nap.
If you want happiness for a day, go fishing.
If you want happiness for a year, inherit a fortune.
If you want happiness for a lifetime, help somebody.

Chinese Saying

Perception plays a part in giving; if you do it because you feel guilted or shamed into it, you are unlikely to feel good about it and therefore won't experience a boost of happiness. It isn't about how *much* you give, but how *good* you feel about giving. Money isn't the only way to contribute to others;

giving your time can be even more valuable than handing over a cheque. The important factor is that it comes from your heart.

Something Bigger Than You

In Precept #4: Change Your Perspective, I wrote about research carried out by Amy Wrzesniewski.

The data she collected during her study of what makes people happy at work revealed three orientations, or ways, that people view the work they do. You may view your work as a job, a career, or a calling. These three orientations are split fairly evenly between the working population.

If you see your work as a job, you are doing it for the money and other benefits it provides. Perhaps it allows you to work only during school hours, or has a salary that allows you to afford the life-style you want.

With a career orientation, you see the work you do as a stepping stone to advancement. If you want to manage your own store one day, you accept that you must work your way up the career ladder.

Those people who see the work they do as a calling believe that their job serves a bigger purpose than what it does just for them and their family. They believe they are part of a bigger picture. In Wrzesniewski's study of hospital janitors, those who saw themselves as caring professionals believed that their work was a calling. They worked for their salary, but enjoyed what they did because it was serving others.

During my teaching career, I experienced all three of these orientations at different times. When I entered my first classroom I was full of future possibilities and saw myself as having a career. I envisioned myself moving up to a department head and vice principal and then maybe to becoming a principal.

After a year or two, I realized that I loved being in the classroom and didn't want to sacrifice that by being an administrator. My orientation had changed to a calling. I saw myself making a difference in the lives of the students I taught, and helping to shape future generations.

When I became a mom, my reason for working took a different direction. My priority became my young children, and although I still enjoyed teaching, my focus was to have as much time as possible with my family. I quit my full-time job at a prep school and found a local part-time position. I hated the work as I felt I was more of a babysitter than a teacher, but I was willing to endure it because it meant I had more time at home. My main purpose in going to work was for the pay cheque and the time it gave me at home. Teaching had become a job for me.

Which orientation did I enjoy the most? Without a doubt, I was happiest when I saw myself as having a calling.

How This Increases Happiness

Studies show that people who perceive that their life has meaning and purpose experience healthy changes at the cellular level.

The need for relatedness that contributes to the Self-Determination Theory applies not only to feeling you belong among your social networks, but also in your larger community. Seeing yourself as being part of a bigger picture helps satisfy your need to feel linked to the world around you. This leads to a higher level of motivation, something many students, young people and adults are lacking.

Peter Warr lists one of the Needed Nine Features of Happiness as having a valued role. If you perceive yourself as being part of a bigger picture, something that is necessary for the well-being of others, you are likely to view yourself as having a valued role.

You may not want a lot of public recognition, but it is important to feel what you do is valuable. There is a lot of variation in what each one of us sees as a valued role. Don't assume that your definition is universal. Your feelings of worth may come from your own value system, the company you work for, or the society you live in. People in any job need to see themselves as valued if they are going to be happy.

Staying at home and looking after young children is very rewarding, but also incredibly hard work. You are on call 24/7, and yet there is no paycheque given to you at the end of each month. Surprisingly, parents who stay home are often happy because they see themselves as having a valued role. What is more important than making sure your children get a good start in their lives?

The Principle

Humans are social creatures, and although you are wired to survive, you are also wired to care about the community you live in. Seeing the things you do as being part of a bigger picture, and taking the time to improve the lives of others and positively change the world around you, is important if you want robust happiness.

Action

1. See yourself as one piece in a larger puzzle

   If you want to increase your self-motivation, see yourself as part of a larger community, or involved in a purpose bigger than just yourself. You are a thread in a tapestry. On your own you are just a thread, together you are a stunning design.

   Create volunteer opportunities for students of all ages. Find opportunities for your children to volunteer their time, or to assist you while you are volunteering.

2. See yourself as part of a team

   Encourage your family or class members to help with chores for the good of the unit, not because they must to earn their allowance or be allowed out for recess.

3. Model the role of a charity-minded person

   Be a volunteer; take time to help people in need, and give to charities and non-profit organizations that have a vision you agree with. Remember, there are more ways to give than just with money.

4. View the work you do as a calling

   View your work as a teacher or parent as a calling. You are teaching and raising the next generation of leaders and change makers.

5. Create a school or family community

Create a school community that everyone feels they are an active part of. The standards they help establish when they are one of the older students in the school will influence those coming up behind them. Design opportunities for students to help others. You don't have to be an academic superstar to effectively help children younger than yourself. Research shows that the best way for anyone to learn is to teach a skill to someone else. Take advantage of this solution which benefits everyone. Make learning a community affair.

Help children and youths develop a habit of doing things for others that do not benefit themselves in any way. As a family, class, grade, or school, support a charity. Make sure you choose something that aligns with the values of the people involved. Children helping other children can make a powerful impression. Try, if possible, to let the students or family members help select the charity. This fits with a need for autonomy and makes the decision more meaningful.

6. Explain to students why the things they are learning are part of the curriculum

Give school skills and assignments context and a reason to be learned. If students understand the purpose of what they are learning, it is easier for them to accept it should be learned. If possible, create assignments that are meaningful for students. You may be able to let them help decide what books to read or topics to research.

7. Make choices that will benefit others, not just yourself

Help your students/children to see they are part of a much bigger community. Their actions make a difference to the environment and society. Be good to the earth and to each other.

Conclusion

It would be very difficult to live your life without giving to others, but do you consciously give without any expectation of personal gain? This is the key to charity that makes you feel happier. If you are looking for a way to take happiness-boosting action, charity work may be a great area to explore. There are many worthy organizations looking for volunteers. Start with one project or block of time, to ensure that the charity or non-profit is a good fit for you. If it isn't, try another one.

If you change the perspective you use to view your work, you may feel more committed to your job and leave each day with a greater feeling of satisfaction. Concentrate on how what you do helps other people. If you are a parent, change the perspective you use to view your parenting duties. Raising well-adjusted, robustly happy children is one of the most valuable contributions you can make to society.

Section IV –
Final Thoughts

Summary of the Precepts

#1 Enjoy the Journey

Life is a journey; happiness comes from being in control of the path you take. When children are very young, they need to be led and guided, but it is important to hand the reins to them as they mature. Start small, but ensure that they have practiced the skills and strategies they need to live a robustly happy life.

Recognizing that everyone has their own trek to take makes it easier to move away from a position of judgement. As long as the choices that other people make are not harming anyone, there is no reason for you to believe you know better. Acceptance is one of the greatest ways to create a nurturing community.

#2 Develop a Growth Mindset

Develop a growth mindset. See failure as an opportunity to learn, and don't think the stumbles you make define you as a person. Failing an exam does not mean you are a failure.

Make sure you praise effort and learning, not natural ability or intelligence. Ensure the words you say encourage yourself and others to adopt a growth mindset, rather than a fixed one. With a growth mindset, you will become a life-long learner. The intelligence you are born with is only the starting point, it's where you go from there that is important.

#3 Be Curious

You are programmed to learn through curiosity. Encourage your students and family to nurture and retain their feelings of inquisitiveness. If you wonder about something, take the time to find out the answer. Keep your eyes open for opportunities to learn more about yourself and the world around you.

Honor questions; don't laugh at or ridicule a query that seems obvious or silly to you. If your students/children feel comfortable asking anything, then they will continue to feel safe admitting they don't know something.

There are very few original questions. If one person doesn't understand something, chances are they aren't alone. I used to tell my students that their questions helped me as a teacher. It allowed me to understand the lessons I hadn't taught clearly enough, and gave me a chance to improve.

#4 Make Decisions and Take Responsibility

It takes courage to make a decision and stand by it, especially if other people disagree with you. It is easier to do with a growth mindset, where you see failure as an opportunity to learn. Model decision making skills, and make sure you openly demonstrate how you take responsibility for their results.

Decision making is a vital skill that improves with practice. Encourage students/children to make decisions and take responsibility for them. Don't provide them with a safety net, but be there to help them learn and recover from the experience if they need you.

#5 Change Your Perspective

Happiness is all about choice. Choose how you are going to react to circumstances, and how you are going to interpret the events you observe. The glass is both half-full and half-empty, you get to choose which version you want to believe.

Take time to demonstrate how different viewpoints can be used to see the same situation. Be mindful of looking for a win-win solution or perspective when other people are involved.

#6 Connect with Others

Humans are hardwired to connect with others. It doesn't matter how introverted you think you are, you still need to have social connections. Don't underestimate the importance of this; nurture your existing relationships, and be willing to invest time to develop new ones.

Social connection is vital for happiness, and as a result schools need to ensure every student feels they are accepted and belong to the community. Take time to get to know each person you teach, and let them get to know you; this is an important piece of the school culture and close family-unit puzzles.

#7 Take Action

Change won't happen unless you choose to act. This is the most important precept if you want to make a difference in the world. How you behave is the example you are setting for the impressionable minds that are watching you. Knowing how to be happy is of no use unless you embody the precepts. Give the people around you a realistic example of what a happy life can look like.

If you find it difficult to act, then it is all the more important to take the plunge. The big difference between most dreams that become reality and those that don't is the willingness of the dreamer to take action. Reading this book won't help change the world unless you are willing to put these philosophies into practice. Don't wait until you feel perfectly prepared; that is just a form of procrastination. Be brave and start now.

#8 Be Part of Something Bigger

Look for a way of seeing yourself as part of a bigger picture. You can focus on your work or personal life, but find a way to help the larger community you live in. This can be at a local, national, or international level. Model this way of thinking and behaving for your students/children.

Give children the chance to see themselves as part of a bigger picture. How can they make a small change in the world? Set goals that have no personal payoff for you, your family or your students. Help them understand that every puddle starts with a single drop of rain.

Getting Started

I hope you feel as motivated to be part of the Modelling Happiness movement as I am. If you are, then it is important that you act. Take small steps. You can't change the world in one day. Even epic journeys start with a single stride.

Start by becoming aware of your thoughts and behaviors. Would you be proud if others copied them? What can you do to adjust?

Choose one precept and think of a single way you can move towards adopting it. Write it down. Create a strategy to make it happen. If you decide your first step is to develop a growth mindset, you might enlist the help of a friend or family member to help you realize when you slip back into a fixed mindset, then change your words, thoughts, or actions to reflect your new way of thinking.

I love to be surrounded by words and quotes that encourage me on my path. Put messages on your desk, pictures on your walls, and post-its on your mirror. It is important to remain conscious of the step you have chosen to take. When you feel you have a handle on that step, choose another one.

Share the precepts with others; this will add accountability to your journey. If your friends, family, students, and colleagues know about your intentions, they will become a network for both support and responsibility. Embody the principles. If you live and believe them, then your enthusiasm will attract others to their magic.

Advice for Schools

> *A teacher affects eternity;*
> *He can never tell where his influence stops.'*
>
> Henry Adams (American Historian)

You have a tremendous amount of impact on the lives of your students. You may never know the effect you have on the children who pass through your classroom, but rest assured that many will remember you. Make sure you inspire them to believe in themselves and the differences they can make in the world. A tiny pebble can start a large ripple.

Every adult in your school, regardless of whether they are part of the teaching staff or not, needs to be modelling these eight precepts if you want to change your school culture to its very core. Support each other and allow opportunities for professional development.

That isn't to say you shouldn't change the culture in your classroom, even if the rest of the school isn't on board yet. Teaching and applying the precepts in your classroom will ensure your students have a safe place to learn. You can be the pebble that starts the ripple in your school.

Use your brilliance as a teacher to find those golden teachable moments. This will happen naturally if you believe in and model the precepts. Be open about your feelings, struggles, and learning opportunities. By sharing a little about how you cope with life, you will create a stronger bond with your students and teach them that everyone's journey has challenges.

Use the vocabulary of the precepts throughout the school. This will make communication and discussion easier for everyone. Don't forget how important understanding is. Include the science behind the precepts whenever it is appropriate. Knowledge is powerful.

Advice for Parents

> *Your children may not be listening to you, but they are definitely watching you.*

As children, we copy the actions of the significant adults in our lives, often without question. So many of the methods I have adopted are the ones I saw my mother exhibit. 'Monkey see, monkey do,' is far more than just an expression. When those little monkeys are looking at you, are they copying behaviors that you want them to adopt?

In T. Harv Eker's book, *Secrets of the Millionaire Mind*, he tells the story of a woman who cuts off the ends of a ham before she cooks it. When her husband asks her why, she says that was the way her mom did it. When her mother arrives for dinner, they ask her why she cut the ends off the ham. She replies by saying that's the way her mom cooked it. They phone Grandma to ask her why she prepared the ham that way, and she told them it was because her pan was too small to hold the ham, so she cut the ends off to make it fit. Without question, each generation followed the same process for cooking a ham, even though it was no longer necessary to do so.

Start by examining your own beliefs and behaviors. Do they fit with the precepts in this book? Model the person you want your children to become. Honor the fact that every family member has their own path to follow and lessons to learn. Saving them from difficult times is not helpful. Let them experience life in all its forms, and be there to help them if they stumble or fall.

Use the vocabulary from the precepts. This common language will make it easier for you to communicate. Don't think that you need to have everything figured out. You are on your own journey of discovery, and will continue to learn throughout your entire life.

Encourage schools to become part of the Modelling Happiness movement, and suggest the Parent Advisory Council/Parent Teacher Association get involved. Having a support system of other parents will make the learning process easier.

Conclusion

Be a light not a judge.
Be a model not a critic.

Stephen Covey

I set out to write a book that would encourage teachers and parents to help improve the mental wellness of the world by modelling what a happy life looks like. Don't be misled into thinking that happiness is something you can capture; it is a philosophy, a way of life, an attitude. By making a commitment to become a happiness model for today's children, youths, and young adults, you will be joining me in this mission to transform the world.

If I had known that I was the key to my own happiness, or had some understanding of emotions and the happiness skills I needed when my life nose-dived, I don't think I would have sunk quite so low. In spite of that, I believe there was a reason for me to take that journey. Mental health issues have always been present, but they are affecting the younger generations more now than ever before. If this book helps just one person, then *Modelling Happiness* will be a success.

You may believe that your students and children are happy, and maybe they are, but is it the sort of happiness that will sustain them during difficult times? Do they understand that they are in control of their own happiness? If not, they are in a very vulnerable position.

As I said in the introduction, this book is about change, choice, and happiness. Only you can change your life into a robustly happy one; the decision is yours. Help others discover the same understanding by becoming a happiness model. Together, we can change the world, one child, one classroom, one family at a time.

www.ingramcontent.com/pod-product-compliance
Lightning Source LLC
LaVergne TN
LVHW090049160826
845672LV00015B/1617